GW00630651

Riding
in a weekend

WITHDRAWN FROM TORBAY LIBRARY SERVICES

Riding
in a weekend

step-by-step techniques to improve your skills

DEBBIE SLY

PHOTOGRAPHY BY KIT HOUGHTON

southwater

This edition is published by Southwater

Southwater is an imprint of Anness Publishing Ltd
Hermes House, 88–89 Blackfriars Road, London SE1 8HA
tel. 020 7401 2077; fax 020 7633 9499
www.southwaterbooks.com; info@anness.com

© Anness Publishing Ltd 1998, 2004

UK agent: The Manning Partnership Ltd,
tel. 01225 478444; fax 01225 478440; sales@manning-partnership.co.uk

UK distributor: Grantham Book Services Ltd,
tel. 01476 541080; fax 01476 541061; orders@gbs.tbs-ltd.co.uk

North American agent/distributor: National Book Network,
tel. 301 459 3366; fax 301 429 5746; www.nbnbooks.com

Australian agent/distributor: Pan Macmillan Australia,
tel. 1300 135 113; fax 1300 135 103; customer.service@macmillan.com.au

New Zealand agent/distributor: David Bateman Ltd, 30 Tarndale Grove, Off Bush Road, Albany,
Auckland; tel. (09) 415 7664; fax (09) 415 8892

All rights reserved. No part of this publication may be reproduced, stored in a retrieval system, or trans-
mitted in any way or by any means, electronic, mechanical, photocopying, recording or otherwise, without the prior written permission of the copyright holder.

A CIP catalogue record for this book is available from the British Library.

Publisher: Joanna Lorenz
Design: Twin
Photographers: Kit Houghton and Susan Ford

Previously published as *Riding Essentials*

10 9 8 7 6 5 4 3 2 1

C O N T E N T S

INTRODUCTION

The close partnership that develops between horse and rider is one of the most rewarding yet challenging that you are ever likely to encounter. Whether your intention is to ride for sport or for pleasure, horse riding is one of the few activities where you are totally reliant on another living creature for your success or downfall.

Perhaps the most frustrating thing about learning to ride is that the experts make it look so simple. The rider appears to be doing nothing as his horse works effortlessly beneath him. This should be the aim of the novice rider – to work in complete harmony with the horse; it comes with practice and determination.

Unfortunately there are no shortcuts that will turn you into a successful rider overnight. It requires practice and experience – the more you ride the more comfortable you will feel on the horse and soon, what once felt awkward and unnatural will become second nature.

The key to successful 'natural' riding is to achieve a balanced, secure seat on the horse so that your hands, legs and bodyweight can act independently to influence the way the horse moves beneath you. This is known as achieving an independent seat. Once acquired, it allows you to use the correct technique to harness and enjoy the full power and grace that the horse can offer you. The following pages offer a step-by-step guide to understanding and influencing the horse. By mastering the essential techniques that form the basis of good horsemanship, you will, with time and practice, be able to fully enjoy all that the horse can offer you.

BEFORE YOU START

If you have never sat on a horse or pony, there will be a lot to take in at first. It will help to have an overall idea of what you want to achieve, and the right language to describe the parts of the horse. It helps to remember that once you have mounted the horse your means of communication are through the use of the legs, seat, hands and voice. You use your legs first and foremost to instruct the horse to do something. The legs create the power, while the hands gently guide the horse in the right direction. You should aim for the same smooth feeling of control as driving a high-performance sports car when riding a horse.

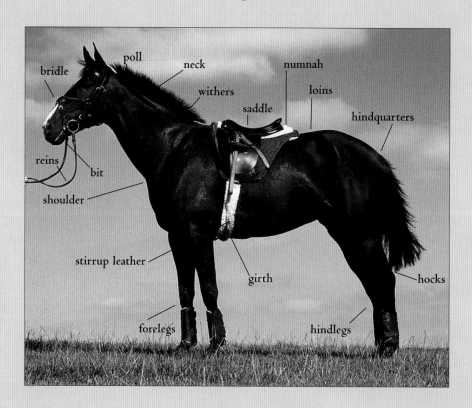

FINDING YOUR WAY AROUND A HORSE

As a beginner, you will usually be taught to ride in a circle around an instructor. The hand and leg on the inside of the circle, i.e. the hand and leg nearer the instructor, are referred to as the inside hand and leg. The hand and leg on the outside of the circle are known as the outside hand and leg. If your inside hand is your left hand, i.e. you are going in an anticlockwise direction, you are said to be riding on the left rein. If you are told to change the rein, this involves turning the horse around and circling in the opposite direction, so that the inside hand is now your right hand, and you are riding on the right rein.

NEAR SIDE, OFF SIDE

Some of the first terms to learn in order to avoid confusion are the words that describe each side of the horse. If you stand facing in the same direction as the horse, his left-hand side is known as the near side, and his right-hand side is known as the off side. The horse is led from the near side; you mount and dismount from the near side. The same terms are used to denote each of the horse's limbs — if a horse is said to be lame on his off fore, this refers to the front leg on the right-hand side.

NATURAL AIDS

Your legs, seat, hands and voice are known as natural aids. Any commands — from walking forwards to performing intricate movements — are achieved by using a combination of these aids. The art of riding lies in learning to feel what the horse is doing underneath you, and understanding how to influence his movements by mastering the subtle interplay of leg, seat and hand.

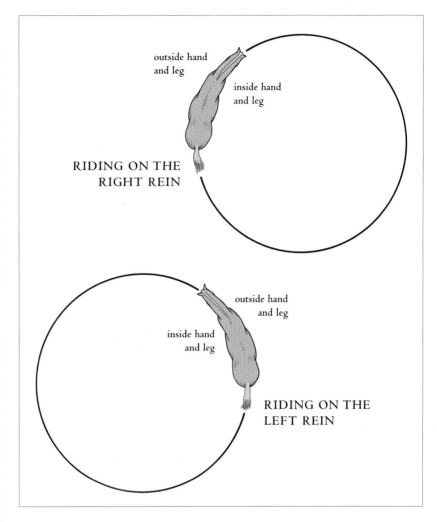

outside hand and leg

inside hand and leg

RIDING ON THE RIGHT REIN

outside hand and leg

inside hand and leg

RIDING ON THE LEFT REIN

ARTIFICIAL AIDS

Natural aids can be backed up with artificial aids — the spur and the whip. The spur is a short stump of blunt metal, worn over the rider's boot just above the heel; the whip is either a short stick or a longer schooling whip.

CONTROLLING THE HORSE

You should aim for the same smooth feeling of control as driving a high-performance sports car when riding a horse. Just as a powerful car responds instantly to a touch on the accelerator, a horse should move forwards as soon as he feels a light squeeze from the rider's leg. Your arms and hands are linked via the reins to the bit in the horse's mouth. This line of contact is all part of your communication with the horse and you must maintain a consistent but soft contact with the mouth. The idea is not to let the reins keep going slack and then tight, but to relax your arms enough to follow what the horse's head and neck are doing whilst keeping a constant feel on the reins.

CLOTHING AND EQUIPMENT

Protective clothing is essential for both horse and rider. Whatever your standard of riding, and no matter how little or often you ride, in the town or in the country-side, your priority must always be to wear equipment that conforms to the highest safety standards. The basic safety requirements are outlined here.

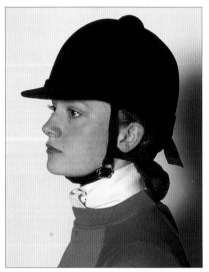

▲ The velvet riding hat is styled on the hunting cap. Always wear a stock – a form of scarf or neck tie – for cross-country riding, because it will support the neck in the case of a fall.

HARD HATS

The first vital item to possess is a hard riding hat – also known as a crash hat or skull cap – of a recognized safety standard. A riding hat must always be worn with a safety harness to hold it in place; a traditional hard hat with an elastic chin strap is almost useless.

Hard hats come in various designs, including the traditional velvet hat with a built-in peak and the crash hat or skull cap as worn by racing jockeys and cross-country riders. Some of the newest styles are lightweight, vented helmets that protect the head while allowing the rider to stay cool. Always replace a riding hat that has suffered a hard blow, either through a fall or by being dropped accidentally. The leading current standards are the European PAS 015 and the American ASTM/SEIF 1163.

▲ The jockey-style crash hat or skull cap (with harness) can be worn on its own or with a silk.

RIDING BOOTS

The right footwear is essential. Long or short boots need to be close-fitting so as not to catch in the stirrup in the event of a fall, and the heel should be small, so that your foot won't get trapped.

▶ If you prefer, cover the jockey-style hat with a "silk"– dark blue or black for the arena, and a colour to match your outfit for cross-country riding.

There is a good range of boots for leisure riding, but for any form of competition riding, the correct turnout is long leather boots or short, leather riding boots, such as jodhpur boots.

TROUSERS

For the sake of comfort, wear trousers designed specifically for riding. Any garment with a thick seam will chafe against your skin, and material that is too thin will wear through.

CHAPS

Chaps are shaped leggings worn with short boots. Half-chaps are worn below the knee and protect the lower leg. They prevent the stirrup leather from rubbing against the rider's calf. Full chaps cover the whole leg and are fastened with a belt around the waist.

BODY PROTECTOR

This is a padded, vest-like garment that is mandatory in most countries for sports such as horse racing and the cross-country phase of horse trials. Wear a body protector over your usual riding top or underneath your clothes.

NECK STRAP

A neck strap is a leather strap hung loosely around the horse's neck. It sits just above the withers and is there for you to hold on to if you lose your balance. The neck strap also prevents the horse from being "jabbed" in the mouth.

▲ Short leather jodhpur boots can be worn with jodhpurs, or with a pair of half chaps to protect the lower leg.

◀ Long riding boots can be made of either rubber or leather.

► Breeches are intended for wear with long riding boots.

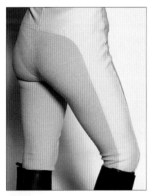

▼ Jodhpurs are usually made of a stretchy material and are designed to be worn with short boots.

▼ Most riders like to wear gloves. Make sure you choose a pair with non-slip palms; otherwise the reins will slip through your fingers.

▲ If spurs are worn, they should be as short as possible and must have a rounded or blunt end. They should never be used by beginners. Do not wear spurs until you have good control of your lower leg or you will spur your horse unnecessarily.

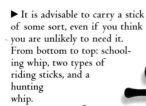

► It is advisable to carry a stick of some sort, even if you think you are unlikely to need it. From bottom to top: schooling whip, two types of riding sticks, and a hunting whip.

UNDERSTANDING HORSES AND PONIES

The first thing that any would-be rider must appreciate is the sheer strength and bulk that a horse or pony represents. Common sense should tell even the most inexperienced person that the relationship between horse and rider cannot possibly be based on force – if it were, the horse would win every time. As a rider, you are totally dependent on the horse's co-operation, and so the partnership between horse and rider is one of mutual respect.

KNOW YOUR PARTNER

Much of the secret behind the successful handling of a horse or pony, either from the ground or from the saddle, is based on the calmness and confidence of the human being in the partnership. So before learning to ride, it is well worth spending time just getting used to being with horses. Most riding schools would be more than happy to accept an offer of help around the yard, and this is a good opportunity to become comfortable around horses.

STAYING CALM

Horses are happiest when handled confidently and positively. They are far more likely to become nervous and unsure if the handler is jittery and tentative. They can feel the tension of a nervous rider.

◀ It is a great advantage to learn to ride at an early age. There are classes for young riders on lead reins at most local gymkhanas.

Horses, like people, have different temperaments, and not every horse will get on in the same way with every person. A sharp, nervous horse will probably not feel comfortable with an equally excitable handler – he is more likely to respond to a quieter personality. An extrovert rider, on the other hand, may inspire confidence and coax a little more effort out of a horse with a more relaxed character.

PRAISE AND PUNISHMENT

Horses or ponies should always be handled firmly but fairly, so that they learn what is expected of them. It is the rider's job to teach the horse what is acceptable and what is not. Always remember that you are the boss.

As with the training of other animals, when a horse does what you require, you reward him; when he disobeys, you quietly reprimand him. It is vital to be consistent in what you ask. It is not fair to hug and kiss him, then turn around and wallop him when he changes position and steps on your toe! Although you may doubt it at the time, the horse would not step on you deliberately.

Your voice is the most valuable form of communication you have. A horse or pony will know from your tone of voice whether you are pleased with him or otherwise. So use your voice to tell the horse when he is behaving well and when he is not. Your commands should be clear and simple: if the horse does something wrong, a stern "No" is often enough to convey this. A long, angry tirade will only confuse the horse, and wear you out. Confine yourself to "No" when the horse is wrong, and "Good boy" or "Good girl" when things are going well. Far too many riders forget to praise the horse for co-operating.

◀ Riding lessons are beneficial and fun once the potential rider has had a chance to master some of the basics.

any establishment where novices are put on badly schooled, bored mounts and stuck in a class with numerous other potential riders, and where inexperienced or incompetent instructors swagger around bawling instructions or criticism. The results of such teaching will be that the new riders will either give up or become aggressive jockeys, oblivious to the reality of true horsemanship.

INDIVIDUAL LESSONS
If you are unable to take lunge lessons, the next best choice is individual rather than group lessons. Once you have mastered some of the basics, riding in a group can be a positive and enjoyable experience, but when learning from scratch, individual attention right at the beginning is unbeatable. This can be arranged at a commercial riding school or equestrian centre, or with a private individual who gives lessons using their own horse and facilities.

QUALIFIED INSTRUCTORS
Ensure that the instructor of your choice has a good reputation both for teaching ability and for being safe and responsible. In most countries there is some form of recognized teaching body and a structured system of examinations for instructors; if you have nobody to advise you, always opt for a registered and approved instructor. But if someone is highly recommended to you by more experienced riders, do not be afraid to try them even if teaching is not their profession – some people are naturally gifted teachers.

WHERE TO LEARN
Some children are lucky enough to be put on a pony before they can even walk. Long before they are in a position to control their ponies off the leading rein, they will have developed a natural seat – a secure balance that is crucial to effective communication with the horse. This is because someone else is in charge of the pony – all the rider has to worry about is staying on board. The same principle can be applied by riding a horse that is being lunged: led in a circle by means of a long rope.

If time and money allow, the older beginner's best investment is a course of lunge lessons at a reputable equestrian centre. The advantages are that you will receive individual attention and, most importantly, you will start to acquire a relaxed seat in the saddle. Lungeing will also give you the opportunity to feel how the horse moves underneath you.

GROUP LESSONS
If contemplating lessons, you would be wise to visit the school before you enrol, or before you pay for your lessons. Avoid

TACKING UP

Tacking up is the process of equipping your horse before mounting. It is essential that this is done correctly — for both you and your horse's safety and comfort. It gives you a few minutes in which to start getting to know your horse as you prepare him for riding.

It is safer to tack up your horse while he is standing still, tied up to a secure post. The order in which the horse is tacked up varies, but any form of boots should be put on first. Check the horse's legs for signs of heat or swelling. This should have been done while the horse was being groomed, but it is good practice to double-check when attaching the boots — there is no point in tacking up and then finding that the horse is lame! If you are sharing tack with another rider, make sure that it is clean and well-fitting.

Whether the saddle or bridle is put on next is a matter for discussion. Some riders put the bridle on first, so that they have better control of the horse should he pull back and break free from his headcollar. Others like to put the saddle on first, so that when the horse's rugs are removed, the saddle goes straight on to a warm back and the horse's muscles will not cool beneath the saddle. On a cold day, a rug should be kept over the horse's back and quarters while you are tacking up.

PUTTING ON THE BRIDLE

1 ◄ While being tacked up or groomed, the horse is usually secured by a headcollar. Before removing the headcollar, put the bridle reins over the horse's head to provide a means of holding him.

2 ▼ Remove the headcollar by lifting the headpiece forward and then gently over the horse's ears.

3 ◄ With one hand holding the horse's nose to keep the head steady, bring the bridle up in front of the face.

4 ◀ Use your right hand to hold the bridle firmly as shown left. Lay the bit over the palm of your left hand and gently lift it up into the horse's mouth. Use your thumb to press the gum in the gap where the teeth finish, which will encourage the horse to open up his mouth.

5 ◀ Once the bit is in place, keep some tension on each side of the bridle to hold it there while you bring the headpiece of the bridle up and over the horse's ears. Do not allow the bit to bang against the teeth as this will make the horse wary next time.

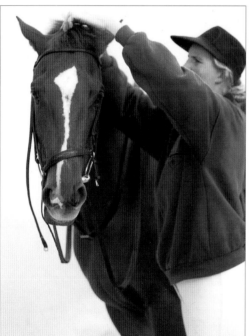

7 ◀ Keep your hand looped through the rein to maintain contact with the horse, and thereby keep control, as you do up the throatlash.

6 ▲ With the headpiece in place, separate the hair of the forelock from the rest of the mane (to let the bridle sit comfortably, cut a small section out of the mane where the headpiece sits). Bring the forelock forward and lift it clear of the browband.

▶

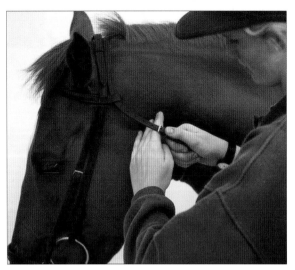

8 ◄ It should not be fastened too tightly: make sure that you can get four fingers between the horse's cheek and the throatlash.

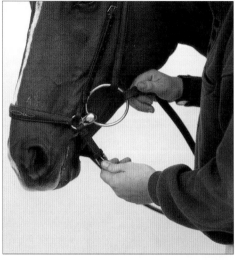

9 ◄ Fasten the noseband – in this case a drop noseband, which does up below the bit rings. A cavesson noseband sits higher up the horse's nose and fastens above the bit rings.

10 ▼ You should be able to fit one finger between the horse's chin and the noseband. Make sure that the noseband is not so tight as to restrict the horse's breathing or hinder the movement of his head. However, a noseband fitted too loosely will irritate the horse.

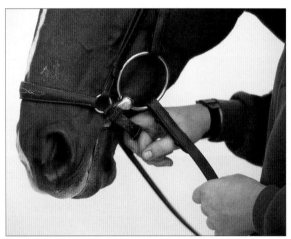

PUTTING ON BOOTS ►

Protective boots reduce the risk of injury. Hold the boot securely in place and fasten the first strap. Then fasten the second strap firmly, to prevent the boot from slipping. Tighten the first strap if it seems looser than the second strap. These boots protect the tendon area as well as the inside of the fetlocks. Many horses are prone to knocking one leg against the inside of the opposite leg – known as brushing – and boots protect the horse from resultant injury.

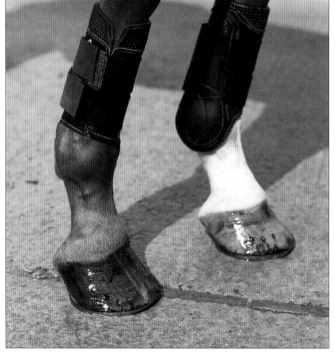

SADDLING UP

1▶ Place a soft, padded numnah (felt or sheepskin cloth) on the horse's back. This acts as a cushion between the horse and the saddle and can relieve pressure points and reduce the risk of rubbing. It is also a warmer layer against the horse's skin than the leather of the saddle.

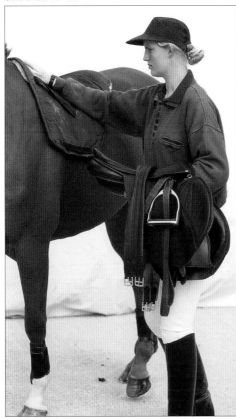

3▶ Use your left hand to lift the numnah so that it is not pulled tight over the horse's withers. It should be tucked up to lie snugly under the pommel of the saddle, clear of the withers.

2▶ Keeping the saddle well clear of the horse's back, lift it so that it is poised in the right position to be lowered on to the back. Lower the saddle into place, making sure that the saddle flap on the off side is lying flat.

4▲ Most of the numnahs available have two straps that hold them in position under the saddle. The first one is usually attached to the girth straps, so pull it over the knee roll of the saddle and put it on the strap before you do up the girth. Make sure that you have not trapped any of the horse's skin or hair on the underside. Otherwise the numnah may pinch the horse, causing constant and painful discomfort all through your ride.

▶

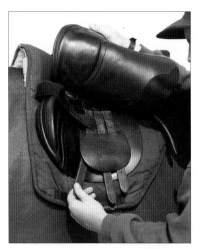

5 ◄ Position the strap above the buckle guard, otherwise you will not be able to pull this down into the correct position. Pull the girth strap out from the buckle guard, thread through the numnah strap, then put the strap back through the buckle guard.

8 ◄ Pull the buckle guard down so that it covers the buckles – otherwise they will gradually wear a hole through the saddle flap.

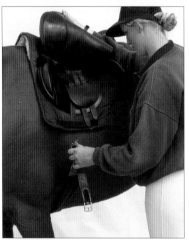

6 ◄ Buckle the girth to the saddle on the off side. Return to the near side, and reach under the horse's belly to catch the girth. Thread the girth buckles through the second securing strap of the numnah and fasten them, one at a time, to each girth strap.

9 ◄ Smooth down under the girth so that there are no wrinkles of skin caught up which might rub. Slide your hand under the girth just clear of the saddle flap and run it down under the horse's belly, taking particular care to smooth any wrinkles in the horse's elbow area.

7 ◄ Gently tighten the girth, one buckle at a time, until you can just squeeze the flat of your hand between the horse's belly and the girth. Fasten the girth equally on each side.

10 ◄ A correctly fitted jumping saddle, with the girth tightened and the stirrups run up so that they do not swing and bang against the horse's sides. A jumping saddle has forward-cut flaps and knee rolls to allow the rider to keep his or her leg on the saddle even when riding with shorter stirrups.

TIGHTENING THE GIRTH

You will need to make a few small adjustments to the tack once you are on board the horse. The first is to tighten your girth. Although this is tightened before you mount, your weight pushing the saddle down on to the horse's back will cause the girth to slacken slightly. Also, many horses push their stomachs out against the initial pressure of the girth, and relax again when their riders are in the saddle.

Only when you are sitting on your horse can you feel if your stirrups are set at a comfortable length for you; they may need adjusting.

It is important to achieve the correct pressure on the girth for the comfort of the horse during the ride, and the right length for the stirrups for your own enjoyment and comfort.

1 ◄ To retighten the girth, put both reins and your stick in your right hand and bring your left leg clear of the saddle flap.

2 ◄ Reach down and lift up the saddle flap so that you have access to the girth straps.

3 ◄ Hold the saddle flap out of the way with your right hand. With your left hand, pull the buckle guard up away from the girth straps and buckles.

▶

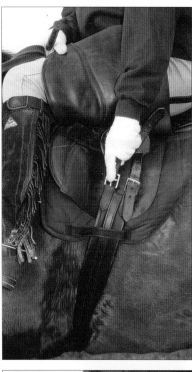

4 ◀ Take hold of the first girth strap and pull it up gently. Use your index finger to press the spike of the buckle through the hole.

6 ◀ Pull the buckle guard down so that it sits snugly over the girth buckles. Put the saddle flap back and return your leg to the correct position.

5 ◀ Do the same to the second girth strap – make sure each is tightened by the same number of holes.

LEADING A TACKED-UP HORSE

◀ When leading a tacked-up horse, stand on the near side and bring the reins over the horse's head. The stirrups should be run up so that they do not swing or bang against the horse's sides. Carry the excess loop of rein and your riding stick in your left hand. Have the stick pointing backwards so that you can give the horse a tap behind the girth if he refuses to walk on. You should always wear a riding hat whenever you lead a horse.

ADJUSTING THE STIRRUP LEATHERS

1 ▶ Once you are in the saddle you may need to adjust your stirrup leathers in order to sit comfortably and correctly. Put the reins and stick in your right hand, and use your left hand to lift the leather flap that covers the stirrup-leather buckle.

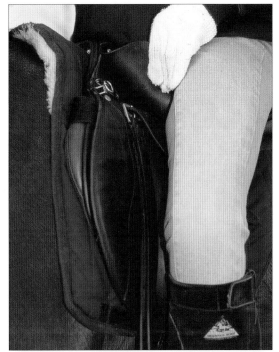

2 ▶ Slide the free end of the stirrup leather out of its keeper if necessary, and then pull it upwards, so that the buckle is released.

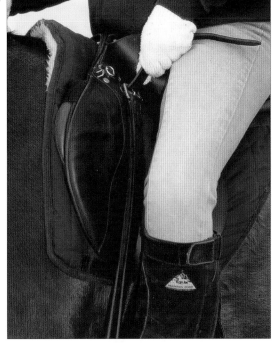

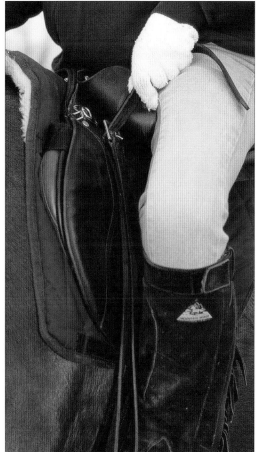

3 ▲ To shorten your stirrup, pull the stirrup leather upwards, as shown. To lengthen your stirrup, put your weight down into the stirrup iron and with your left hand allow the stirrup leather to slide back down through the stirrup bar. A learner should opt for a medium length leather that will allow you to sit in a comfortable and balanced position. A longer leather is usually reserved for jumping and dressage events.

▶

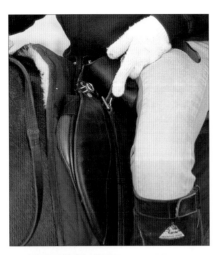

4◄ When the stirrup is at the required length, push the buckle back through the appropriate hole.

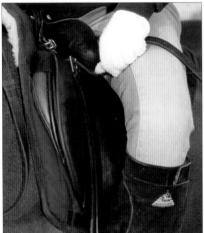

5◄ Make sure the stirrup leather buckle slides back into position, hard up against the stirrup bar.

6◄ Push the free end of the stirrup leather back through the keeper.

7◄ Ensure that the leather is lying flat before repeating the procedure for the right stirrup.

8◄ Each stirrup leather should be turned outwards in order to position the stirrup iron so that your foot can go into it. This allows the stirrup leather to curve smoothly across the inside of your leg. To put your right foot (off-side foot) in the stirrup iron, give the leather a quarter turn in a clockwise direction. For the left (near-side) foot, turn the stirrup leather in an anti-clockwise direction.

HOLDING THE REINS

The reins are an important line of communication with the horse. Imagine that the rein is an extension of your arm and that your hands are attached directly to the bit in the horse's mouth. Be firm, yet gentle: a horse's mouth is an extremely sensitive area.

1 ◄ Hold the reins by allowing them to lie across the palm of your hand. The end that comes from the horse's mouth passes between your third and fourth fingers.

3 ◄ This picture shows you how to hold a stick as well as your reins. When your thumb and fingers close back around the rein and stick, they are held safely in place.

2 ◄ It rests over the top of your first finger and is held in place by closing your thumb and fingers. You can lengthen the reins by relaxing the tension in your hand and letting them slip through your fingers.

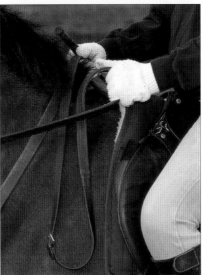

4 ◄ Always hold both hands at the same height: just above the withers and a few inches apart. A straight line should run from your elbow to your arm, wrist and hand and rein to the horse's mouth. This hand and arm position allows you to maintain a soft, elastic but consistent contact with the horse's mouth.

MOUNTING

It is essential to learn how to mount correctly from the ground but, as a general rule, it is far less stressful on the horse's back to use a mounting block or be given a leg-up.

MOUNTING FROM THE GROUND

Many accidents occur when riders are attempting to mount. If you do mount from the ground, an assistant should stand on the far side of the horse, with their hand in the stirrup iron to apply a counter-weight as you swing up. This helps to reduce the amount of twisting and pulling on the horse's spine.

1◄ Before you attempt to get on your horse, you will need to put the reins back over the head, and to let down the stirrups.

2◄ As you pull the stirrup irons down, keep them away from the horse's sides so that they don't knock him. When they are fully down, place them gently back against the horse's sides.

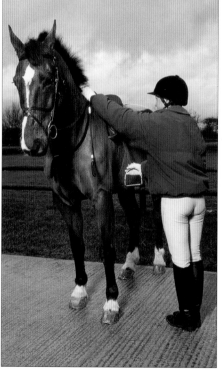

3▲ Stand on the near side of the horse, facing his tail, and put both reins in your left hand. It helps to loop a finger through the neck strap and hold on to a little piece of the mane.

4◄ Take the stirrup iron in your right hand and turn it to face you. The stirrup should be turned clockwise, so that once you are mounted the stirrup leather lies correctly against your leg.

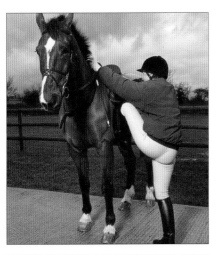

5 ◀ Lift your left leg and place your foot in the stirrup iron. Put your right hand on the seat of the saddle.

8 ◀ At this point start to swing your right leg over the back of the horse. Bring your right hand to the front of the saddle and rest it on either the pommel or the horse's neck to help you support and balance your upper body.

6 ◀ Push with your right leg to spring off the ground and, at the same time, reach to the far side of the saddle with your right hand.

9 ◀ As your right leg starts to come down over the off side of the horse, take your weight on your hands and arms so that you don't just flop down in the saddle. Lower your seat gently into the saddle.

7 ◀ Once you are high enough off the ground, you will be able to grip the far side of the saddle with your right hand and this will help you to balance. Keep bringing your right leg up until it is clear of the horse's back and hindquarters.

10 ◀ Voilà! You are now mounted on your horse. Put your right foot in the stirrup and then take up a rein in each hand.

GETTING A LEG-UP

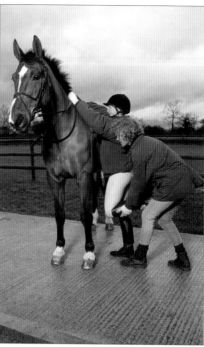

3 ◄ Sink your body weight down into your right leg, and when your helper gives the command be ready to spring up in the air off your right leg.

1 ▲ If someone is going to give you a leg-up on to your horse, stand on the near side, facing the saddle. Take both reins and your stick in your left hand, making sure that you carry the stick down over the off-side shoulder of the horse – otherwise you will hit your helper in the face with it as you mount! Rest your left hand on the horse's neck or on the pommel of the saddle, and reach up with your right hand so that it is resting near the back of the saddle.

2 ▲ Bend your left leg up from the knee, so that your helper can take hold of it firmly with both hands.

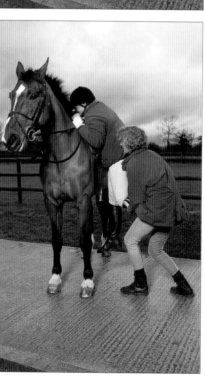

4 ◄ As you spring up off your right leg, your helper will support you by lifting your left leg. Take your weight on your hands, so that you are supporting your upper body and are in full control of the moment when you want to swing your right leg over the horse's back.

USING A MOUNTING BLOCK

5 ◄ As you swing your right leg over the horse's back you will need to transfer your right hand from the back of the saddle to either the pommel or the top of the saddle flap on the off side. Make sure you continue to support your upper body on both your arms.

6 ◄ With your weight on your arms, you can now lower your seat down gently into the saddle.

▲ It is far less stressful for both you and your horse to get aboard with the aid of a special mounting block. A specially designed mounting block is the best option, but a low wall will do just as well. Make sure that whatever you use is stable and sturdy – if the horse moves away suddenly, you may topple off! Lead the horse alongside the mounting block so that the near side is parallel to the block. Use the stirrup to mount in the normal way – carefully bringing your right leg over the horse's back (see Mounting). Because you are that much higher off the ground, there is less strain on the horse's back when you step up into the stirrup.

DISMOUNTING

Before you start riding, you must learn to dismount correctly and safely. Do not be tempted to follow the dangerous example of cowboys and Indians in Wild West movies by flinging your leg over the front of the saddle or the consequences may be painful!

GETTING OFF

Dismounting must be performed slowly and smoothly without startling the horse. If he throws his head up, you will be knocked off backwards, or a sudden action may cause the horse to jump or bolt. Always remove both feet from the stirrups, lean forward, and swing your right leg up and over behind the saddle. Check before you dismount that the ground is safe and free of obstacles.

1 ◄ Prepare to dismount by taking both feet out of the stirrups and putting your reins and stick in your left hand.

2 ► Rest both hands on the pommel of the saddle or on the horse's neck. Lean your upper body forward.

3 Swing your right leg up and over the horse's back.

5 Allow both your legs to drop to the ground together. Bend your knees as you land to absorb the impact.

4 Swing your left leg back and out slightly so that it meets your right leg on the near side of the horse. Use your hands on the saddle to help support your body.

6 Straighten up and you are ready to run up your stirrups, take the reins over your horse's head, and lead him back to the stable.

THE CLASSICAL POSITION

The key to successful riding is to attain what is commonly known as "an independent seat". This is the ability to sit securely and centrally in the saddle, while leaving your legs and hands free to communicate with the horse. It is achieved through the classical position. An independent seat means being able to keep your balance in all paces without gripping with your legs or hanging on by the reins. Only then can your legs, seat and hands be used independently of each other to ask the horse to perform some of the more elaborate and enjoyable movements that he can offer you.

PERFECT POSTURE: THE CLASSICAL POSITION

The classical position is the position that the rider assumes when she first mounts the horse. She sits tall and centrally in the saddle; you should be able to imagine a straight line running from the rider's ear, down through the shoulder and hip to the heel. Similarly, you should be able to draw another straight line from the rider's elbow, through the hand and wrist and down the rein to the bit. The rider's knee should be relaxed so that her body weight can drop down into her heels.

Straight line from rein to bit

Straight line from wrist to rein

Straight line from ear to shoulder

Body is tall in saddle

Straight line from elbow to hand

Straight line from hip to heel

Knees are relaxed

Weight dropped down to heels

TECHNIQUE
AN INDEPENDENT SEAT

By practising the ideal position on the ground, you can start to get a good feel for what you are aiming at, before adding the complication of the horse's body moving underneath you. Similarly, while sitting on the stationary horse you can be shown how to follow the movement of his head and neck, so that you do not restrict the horse or harm him by pulling too harshly on the reins in an attempt to keep your balance.

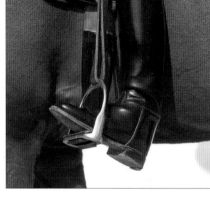

◀ Balance your foot centrally in the stirrup, with the stirrup tread positioned under the ball of your foot and your weight lowered straight down into your heel.

1 ◀ If you sit a child on a pony bareback, her leg position will automatically be long and low as required for the classical position.

2 ◀ As soon as a saddle is introduced, note how the child adopts an armchair seat. Riding bare-back might be the best way to acquire a natural classical seat, but is widely considered to be unsafe.

▲ See how the rider appears to be standing with her knees bent, rather than sitting on the saddle. Note how you can trace a straight line through the rider's ear, shoulder, hip and heel. Another straight line runs from the elbow, down through the wrist and hand to the rein and eventually to the bit in the horse's mouth.

EXERCISE
SOFT CONTACT

One of the secrets of sympathetic and effective riding is to learn how to maintain a soft but constant contact with the horse's mouth whilst allowing him to move his head and neck freely. Soft contact of the reins against the mouth is essential when using the reins as aids – to make the horse do as you wish.

1▶ How not to sit! Do not allow your weight to fall on to the back of your bottom as if you were sitting on a chair. Note how, when this happens, the rider's lower leg swings forward and becomes ineffective as a result.

1▲ Make sure that the horse is fully tacked-up and ready to go. Take up a rein in each hand and ask a friend to hold the rein further down towards the horse's mouth.

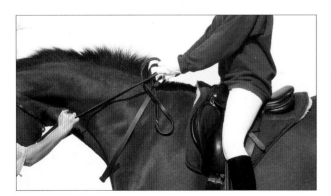

2▲ Ask your friend to mimic the movement of the horse's head and neck by drawing the rein forwards and then releasing it. Concentrate on maintaining a straight line from your elbow, through your wrist and hand down the rein. Keep your elbows and wrists soft and relaxed, and allow your whole arm, from the shoulder down, to be moved by the pull on the reins.

2◀ Do not pitch your weight forward as this prevents you from sitting properly and using your legs correctly – and it is painful! Note how this position causes the lower leg to slide back.

TECHNIQUE
USING THE HANDS

Never forget that your hands are attached via the reins to a large piece of metal in the horse's mouth. The horse's mouth is soft and sensitive, and you must never be harsh with your hands.

"REINS OF SILK"

One of the most important ideas to grasp is that your hands belong to the horse's mouth. Although a light contact must be kept, so that you communicate with the horse, that contact should be elastic. Your hands must follow the movement of the horse's head and neck. You should feel as if you are shaking hands politely with someone; there is equal pressure and movement from each party. An old Spanish proverb suggests that "you should ride as if with reins of silk". This is achieved by keeping the whole arm relaxed, from the shoulder through the elbow to the hand.

POSITION OF HANDS

The position of the hands, and their closeness to the withers, depends upon the horse's head carriage. There should be a straight line from the elbow, through the wrist, down the rein to the bit; so if the horse is working with his head quite low, the hands must be carried a little lower and to either side of the withers in order to keep a straight line. When the horse is working in a rounder outline, the hands can be a little higher; if you are riding a well-schooled horse, who carries his head and neck higher still, your hands should be a few inches above the withers.

1 ◀ You must adjust your arm position, following the horse's head and neck, so that you maintain an imaginary straight line from your elbow, through your wrist and hand, down the rein to the bit. This horse is working in a good outline in trot and you can see how the rider maintains a straight line.

2 ▶ When you encourage the horse to stretch and lower his neck, you must still keep the straight line at all times. Allow your arms and elbows to be drawn forwards and down to maintain the line.

3◄ Here the horse is working with more pronounced flexion and bend through the neck. In this case, you should raise your forearms and hands slightly to maintain the line.

POSSIBLE PITFALLS

1► A common fault is to have stiff, straight arms and to turn the wrists and hands outwards. The harsh appearance of this position underlines how it would prevent a sympathetic contact with the horse.

2▲ A similar error is to position your hands so that the thumbs are pointing downwards. Again this makes it impossible to maintain a soft, consistent contact through the reins with the horse's mouth.

TECHNIQUE
USING THE LEGS

Your legs should hang long and relaxed around the horse's sides, with no tightness in the knee joints. It is the inside calf that squeezes against the horse to move either forwards or sideways.

CORRECT STIRRUP LENGTH

Check that your stirrup length is correct by allowing each leg to hang free. You should then only need to turn your toe up slightly to find the stirrup. This may pull on your thigh and calf muscles. Until your muscles have strengthened sufficiently, ride with the leg in as long a position as remains comfortable.

KNEES

Keep your knee joint relaxed and let it fall away from the saddle slightly, to allow the leg to hang correctly. You should not grip with the knees, or you will push your seat up and out of the saddle. Equally, if you hold your knees tightly against the saddle, you cannot squeeze the horse's sides with your legs. The knee and the toe must be turned slightly outwards to allow the inside of the calf to press against the horse's sides.

LOWER LEG

Resist the temptation to allow the lower leg to be drawn back and upward away from the girth. For some movements, such as turning or controlling the horse's hindquarters, the lower leg is placed a few inches further back behind the girth. The weight must be kept in the heel, the knee and toe turned out slightly, and legs squeezed inwards, not backwards.

1 ▶ To find the correct stirrup length that will allow you to adopt the classical position, sit deep in the saddle and allow your legs to hang long and loose without putting them in the stirrups.

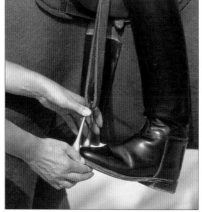

2 ▲ Ask a friend to adjust the stirrup leather so that you need only turn up your toe to find the stirrup iron. It may be some time before you can ride comfortably with such a long stirrup length, because your muscles will need to become supple and stretch, but this is the position you are seeking to achieve.

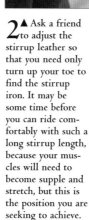

3 ◀ To apply your leg aids correctly, you need to be aware of what your lower leg is doing. When the horse is moving at the desired pace, keep your legs gently in contact with his sides, but do not do anything. The lower leg and the knee joint should remain soft and relaxed.

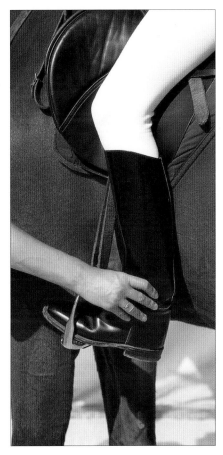

4◄ When you wish to apply a leg aid, simply squeeze your lower leg inwards. Allow your knee to come slightly away from the saddle, so that your lower leg can close in against the horse's side. Your weight remains gently pushed down into your heel. Again you can get a feel for this by asking a friend to push your leg inwards against the horse's sides. Until your muscles are used to this movement it will seem difficult, and you will not be able to apply a very strong leg aid.

I▲ This is a bad leg position: see how the lower leg is pushed forward and away from the horse's sides. It usually occurs when the rider adopts an armchair seat in the saddle and it causes the leg aids to be incorrectly applied.

2▶ Instead of squeezing inwards, this rider has drawn her lower leg back. As a result, her weight has come out of her heel and her heel is higher than her toe. At this point the stirrup iron can easily slip off the foot. This leg aid will not work: the lower leg simply brushes backwards across the horse's side and is not applied to the more sensitive area just behind the girth. With the rider's leg in this position, the horse will think you want him to move his hindquarters to the side. He will not realize that you are asking him to go forwards, and will become confused.

EXERCISE

LUNGEING

A good way to encourage balance and an independent seat is to be lunged, or led in a circle by a trainer holding a lunge rein, which is a long rein about 10 m (33 ft) long. The handler can control the horse's speed and direction, leaving you free to concentrate on your position. It is important that the horse you ride is calm, and that the handler is capable and experienced. A lungeing cavesson should be used over the horse's usual bridle. This is like a padded headcollar with a reinforced noseband that has rings attached to take the lunge line. The handler should maintain a position that allows the lunge line, the lungeing whip and the horse to form a triangle, and lungeing should be carried out in both directions. Lessons should not last for more than 30 minutes, and horse and rider should be allowed rest periods during the exercise.

THE VOICE AS AID
The voice, rather than the lunge whip, aids the horse to move forwards. The lunge whip should only be used as a back-up to the voice, as a last resort if the horse does not respond, and should be moved quietly so that the horse does not suddenly shoot forwards.

THE RIGHT SURFACE
Lungeing should always take place on a secure surface. Hard, rutted, deep or wet surfaces are likely to injure or strain a horse's tendons.

LUNGE LESSONS

1 ◄ Sit securely on the horse, in the classical position. Make sure that your ear, shoulder, hip and heel are all in a line, with equal weight placed on the seat bones. Raise your arms to chest height and extend them to the sides, as shown. Keep your head and arms steady and balanced. As you move, keep looking ahead.

2 ◄ The handler keeps a contact with the horse via the lunge line. The lunge whip can be used behind the horse's hindquarters to encourage him forwards, or flicked towards his shoulder to keep him out on the circle. Both you and the handler should wear a riding hat; the handler should also wear gloves.

HOLDING THE LUNGE LINE

1 ◀ It is important that whoever is going to lunge you knows how to do this safely and correctly. One of the biggest risks to the handler is getting his or her hands trapped in the lunge line should the horse panic and try to run away. The safest way to hold the lunge line is not to loop it around your hand but to lay it across your palm. Do not put your hand through the loop that lies at the end of most lunge lines.

2 ◀ Fold the lunge line in equal loops backwards and forwards across the palm of your hand. Continue to loop the line until it is the desired length, i.e. you are at the distance you want to be from the horse.

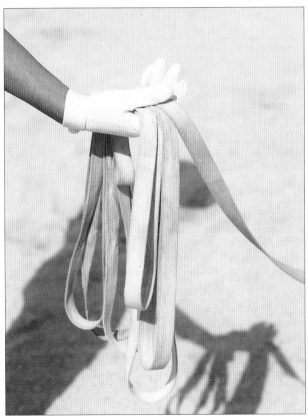

3 ◀ Now you can close your hand around the loops and keep a contact with the horse as he moves. If you want to let more lunge line out so that the horse can work on a larger circle, just open your hand and allow one loop to fall away. If the horse did panic and pull away, you could close your hand tight around the line to try and stop him. But if he has built up too much speed and is determined to escape, the lunge line will be pulled free of your hand without dragging you along or tearing off your fingers.

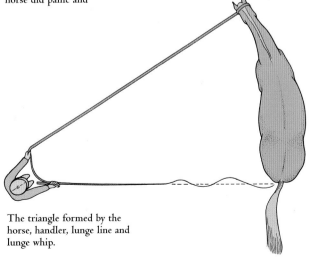

The triangle formed by the horse, handler, lunge line and lunge whip.

EXERCISE

TO STRENGTHEN YOUR BODY

1 ◀ Practise riding without stirrups. To help build up your confidence and balance, spread your arms out to either side.

2 ▲ To strengthen and supple your upper body, twist first round to the left . . .

3 ◀ . . . and then back to the right.

A STRONG BODY

A strong body is essential for a good rider. A strong back in particular will improve your posture and help to achieve the perfect classical position.

EXERCISE

PRACTISING THE CLASSICAL POSITION

1 ◄ You can practise the classical riding position on the ground. First stand straight, with your legs about 60 cm (2 ft) apart, and your arms bent at the elbow as if you were holding the horse's reins.

2 ► Keeping your whole body straight and upright, simply bend your knees slightly. Your position on a horse should be as if you were standing with your knees bent, rather than as if you were sitting in a chair.

3 ► The classical position viewed from the front, showing how the rider's legs would completely encompass the body of the horse. This position allows the leg to support the horse at all times, and enables you to communicate with the horse through your leg aids.

EXERCISE

TO STRETCH YOUR THIGHS

► Practise this simple exercise to help stretch the thigh muscles. Bring your feet up under your bottom and hold them in position with a hand around each ankle. This will also encourage you to keep your shoulders up and straight, and will automatically put your seat in the correct position in the saddle. When you take your stirrups back after this exercise, you may feel that you want to lengthen the stirrup leathers. This is a good sign and is the start of the path towards attaining the classical position.

WALKING

The first thing you will notice when a horse walks is just how much the horse moves underneath you. As each shoulder or hindquarter swings the appropriate leg forward, you will feel it. The walk is described as a four-time pace because the horse moves each leg individually; if you listen to the footfalls, you hear four separate hoofbeats. Each pace that the horse can offer you — walk, trot, canter and gallop — will give a different sensation of speed and motion. To the outside eye, horse and rider should appear to be moving as one.

PERFECT POSTURE: WALKING

In walk the rider must maintain the classical position described earlier despite the fact that the horse is now moving underneath you. By keeping that imaginary straight line through the ear, shoulder, hip and heel, the rider will remain in an effective and balanced position. Your lower back and hips must be relaxed so that they can be gently rocked backwards and forwards by the movement of the horse's hindlegs. Your arms should remain relaxed so that they can follow the movement of the horse's head and neck as he walks. Your weight, as always, should be dropped down into your heel.

Straight line from ear to shoulder

Arms are relaxed

Lower back is relaxed

Hips are relaxed

Straight line from hip to heel

Weight dropped down into heel

TECHNIQUE
ABSORBING MOVEMENT

Don't be tempted to follow the exact movement of the horse with your body to absorb movement. This looks unco-ordinated, and it is also uncomfortable.

A BALANCED SEAT

Visualize your seat as belonging to the saddle which, in turn, belongs to the horse's back. The saddle will mimic the movement of the horse's back and you should imagine that your seat is glued to the saddle. Sit deep in the saddle, with your weight taken equally on each seat bone. Imagine that your legs have been cut off about halfway down the thigh; therefore it is the top half of the thighs and the seat itself which embrace the saddle. Sitting up straight and keeping the shoulders balanced above the hips sinks your weight down into the saddle. This allows the legs to hang long and loose around the horse's sides, with the feet supported gently by the stirrups.

THE HORSE MOVES YOU

Keep the elbows soft and relaxed and the shoulders still. The arms follow the movement of the horse's head and neck. The only part of your body that is free to move is the area between your hips and your ribcage which is rocked gently forwards and backwards by the move-ment of the horse.

Remember that the horse moves your body, and so your body must remain relaxed to allow it to be moved by the horse. Do not create any unnecessary movement yourself – this is most likely to happen if your body is tense.

MOVING WITH THE HORSE

1 ◀ At walk, allow your hips and stomach to be rocked gently for-wards and back by the push of the horse's hind-quarters beneath you. Maintain a straight line from the elbow, through the lower arm, and down the rein to the bit.

2 ◀ Keep a light but constant contact with the horse's mouth by allowing your arms to follow the natur-al movement of the horse's head and neck as he walks.

TECHNIQUE
CHANGING PACE

TRANSITIONS

Changing pace on a horse, whether it be from halt to walk, or from trot to canter etc., is known as performing a transition. Like changing gear in a car, whether you are increasing or decreasing pace, it should appear smooth and effortless.

Transitions are achieved by a subtle combination of hand and leg movement. Use your lower leg to activate the horse's hindquarters, which is where the power comes from. Your hands can then guide that power in whichever direction you wish, through the reins.

REFINING THE USE OF THE LEGS AND HANDS

To walk forwards, squeeze your legs against the horse's sides and allow your hands and arms to be drawn forwards. If the horse ignores you, give him a sharper nudge with your heels. If this is ignored, give him a tap with the schooling whip or stick behind your lower leg. If you have to do this, you must be very quick to keep the soft forward movement of the hands. The horse may jump forwards if he is tapped with the whip, and he must not then be punished by being pulled in the mouth. Remember to reward the horse for obeying and going forwards. With practice, a squeeze with your legs will be sufficient.

To halt the horse, squeeze the legs but do not allow your hands to be drawn forwards so much. The horse will realize that his forward movement is being blocked and will either slow down or shorten the steps he is taking.

1 ◄ Once the horse is walking at the required speed, the rider's legs should remain softly in contact with the sides of the horse

2 ◄ The hands and legs are not used actively until the rider wants to alter the pace. In the meantime the rider allows the movement of the horse to dictate the degree to which her body moves, to keep in balance with the horse.

TECHNIQUE
CHANGING DIRECTION AT WALK

You cannot continue in a straight line forever, so once you are confident with forward movement you must be able to change direction. When the legs are used together to control the horse, either on or fractionally behind the girth, and the hands are also moving together, the horse is kept in a straight line.

CORNERING

To go around a corner, or to turn, the horse has to bend through his body. In order to achieve this, you must use your hands and legs individually. If you allow one leg to slide further back behind the girth, this will make the horse move his hindquarters away from the leg in question: if your right leg is used behind the girth, the horse will be encouraged to move his quarters across to the left, and vice versa. So, to make the horse turn, use one leg in the normal place to encourage him to keep moving forwards, and use the other leg further back behind the girth to control the hindquarters.

SMOOTH AND GENTLE

The horse should never be turned sharply. Any turn should be seen as part of a circle, so to turn right, think about circling away to the right. Then the right hand and leg are referred to as being on the inside, while the left hand and leg are now on the outside. Remember that the horse will obey your commands more readily if they are controlled and considered, not jerky or unexpected.

TURNING RIGHT

1 ▲ Begin to turn off a straight line and away to the right by moving the right hand a few inches away from the withers, towards the right. This is called opening the hand, and it invites the horse to turn his head and neck gradually to the right in preparation for the turn.

2 ▲ Use the inside (right) leg on the girth to keep moving forwards; use the outside (left) leg behind the girth to stop the hindquarters swinging too far to the left. Soften the left hand and arm to retain the bend. The right hand stays to the right of the withers, inviting the horse to move that way.

▲ Notice how gradual and gentle the turn to the right is. There is very little movement of the horse's head from one step to the next. The movement should never be sudden or vigorous.

3 As soon as the horse has turned as far round to the right as you require, return your hands and legs to their normal position.

4 A closer view of hand and leg as the turn begins. The inside (right) hand moves a little to the right of the withers –

opening the hand; the inside (right) leg remains on the girth, encouraging the horse to move forwards at a steady pace.

5 The outside (left) hand softens so that the horse can bend his head and neck away to the right, whilst the outside (left) leg is used behind the girth to control the degree to which the hindquarters move.

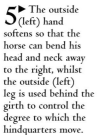

TURNING LEFT

1 ◀ To turn left from a walk, open the inside (left) hand a few inches to the left to invite the horse to turn his head and neck in that direction.

AIDS FOR TURNING

When turning either right or left, the legs and body are the most important aids. The hands should be used as little as possible. Resist tugging at the reins to move the horse into the direction you want.

2 ▶ Soften the outside (right) hand forwards to allow the horse to turn away to the left, while you slide the outside (right) leg back behind the girth to control the swing of the hindquarters.

3 ▶ As soon as the horse is heading in the required direction, return your hands and legs to the normal position.

4 ◀ A closer view shows hand and leg work simultaneously to begin the turn. Open the inside (left) hand to the left to ask the horse to turn his head and neck to the left, while you use the inside leg on the girth.

5 ▶ Allow the outside (right) hand to soften forwards to enable the horse to turn away to the left, while at the same time you use the outside leg behind the girth to control the hindquarters.

RIDING FORWARDS IN A STRAIGHT LINE

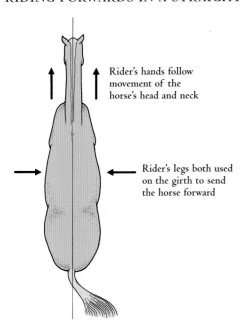

Rider's hands follow movement of the horse's head and neck

Rider's legs both used on the girth to send the horse forward

BENDING TO ALLOW THE HORSE TO TURN RIGHT

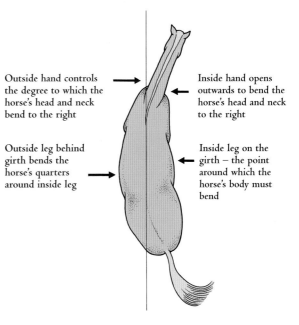

Outside hand controls the degree to which the horse's head and neck bend to the right

Inside hand opens outwards to bend the horse's head and neck to the right

Outside leg behind girth bends the horse's quarters around inside leg

Inside leg on the girth – the point around which the horse's body must bend

EXERCISE

HALT TO WALK AND WALK TO HALT

1 ◄ At halt, keep a light contact with the horse's mouth and let the legs hang long and loose by the horse's sides. The lower leg is in contact with the horse but is not actively doing anything. Note how a straight line is maintained from the shoulder to the hip to the heel. This rider's position would be better still if she kept her chin up – a common fault is the tendency to look down, which curves the back.

2 ◄ To go forwards to walk, squeeze both legs against the horse's sides. Allow the hands and arms to go forward to follow the movement of the horse's head and neck. Once the horse is walking forwards, allow your legs to relax against the horse's sides. Your arms and hands are drawn gently forwards and back by the movement of the horse's head and neck, led by the horse. Do not pull back on the reins.

3 ◄ To prepare to return to halt, squeeze your legs inwards against the horse's sides and, at the same time, reduce the degree to which you allow your arms to follow the movement of the horse's head and neck. On a well-schooled horse, this very slight blocking of the free forward movement will be enough to halt the horse.

4 ▶ On a less responsive horse, you will have to continue reducing the degree to which the hands follow the horse's head and neck to the point where they are held still, which will completely block the forward movement. As soon as the horse halts, soften the hands as much as the horse will allow whilst remaining at halt. Until the horse halts, your legs should stay actively against the horse's sides, gently pushing him up into the hands. Once he has halted, your legs relax and remain gently in contact with the horse's sides.

POSSIBLE PITFALL

◀ If you do nothing with your legs and simply pull on the reins in an effort to slow down, you can see what happens: the horse resists the request to slow down and throws his head and neck in the air in order to fight the pull of the rider; this is described as the horse hollowing against the rider. The whole picture looks tense and uncomfortable. You must first ask with the legs, and then only use as much hand as is absolutely necessary to achieve the desired result.

TROTTING

When the horse trots, you can rise out of the saddle with each stride, in time with the beat of the trot, a technique known as the rising trot, or you can sit deep in the saddle the whole time — which is known as the sitting trot. Both trots are two-time paces — if you listen to the hoofbeats, you hear only two footfalls within each complete stride as the horse moves his legs in diagonal pairs. The outside hind and the inside foreleg move forwards together; this is followed by a brief period of suspension, and then the inside hindleg and outside foreleg move forwards as a pair.

PERFECT POSTURE: RISING TROT – UP

This posture has two parts – up and down. The rider sits and rises in time to the horse's up-and-down movement. The horse's hindlegs push the rider into the rise – it is the horse that moves the rider, not vice versa.

Shoulders are slightly forward

Elbow angled

Hips and stomach swing upwards and forwards

Hands are still and in constant position

Weight drops into heels

PERFECT POSTURE: RISING TROT – DOWN

As you rise just allow your weight to drop down into the heel, and let your hips and stomach swing upwards and forwards. By keeping your weight in your heels you should be able to support the position of your upper body and allow it to be lowered back into the saddle gently.

Shoulders still slighly forward

Angle of elbow moves with rhythm of horse

Hands remain in constant position

Hips and stomach swing upwards and forwards

Downward beat lowers seat back into saddle

Weight remains dropped into heels

TECHNIQUE
RISING TO THE TROT

When trotting, the horse springs from one diagonal pair of legs to the other. To rise to the trot, allow the spring from one pair of legs going forwards to lift your seat out of the saddle. The seat returns to the saddle as the other pair of legs springs forwards. So as the horse moves each pair of legs in a one-two, one-two, one-two beat, you are sitting and rising to the same beat: up-down, up-down.

RISING ON THE CORRECT DIAGONAL

When riding in rising trot in a circle, you should rise in time with a particular diagonal pair of the horse's legs. Look down and watch the horse's outside shoulder for a few minutes once you are in trot. You should be rising out of the saddle as the outside shoulder goes forwards. As it comes back, you should sit again.

The horse will find it easier to balance on a turn or circle if the rider is in the saddle when the inside hindleg and the outside foreleg are touching the ground. Because the legs move in diagonal pairs, this is achieved by sitting as the outside shoulder comes back, and rising as it goes forwards. When you change the rein and circle in the opposite direction, it follows that you must also change diagonal, i.e. rise as the new outside shoulder goes forwards. Changing the diagonal is achieved by sitting for an extra beat before rising again. Instead of sit-rise, sit-rise, you sit-rise, sit-sit-rise, and this puts you on the correct diagonal once more.

▶ You can practise rising to the trot when the horse is stationary. Sit in the classical position, with the knee joints in particular as long and relaxed as possible. Keeping the lower legs as still as you can, concentrate on allowing just your hips and stomach to swing forwards.

2 ◀ Raise your seat only enough to allow the seat bones to be clear of the saddle. Then allow your hips to return lightly to the normal sitting position. Your shoulders and arms remain still – think of allowing your hips and stomach to swing forwards and up towards your elbows.

▶ Don't allow your shoulders to tip forwards. This puts you off balance and you are likely to rest your hands on the horse's neck in an effort to regain equilibrium. When the hands are on the neck, they cannot keep a soft and continuous contact with the horse's mouth. Do not make the movement too aggressive. Try to relax so that your hands can stay soft and still – otherwise you will pull uncomfortably on the mouth of the horse, as you rise up and down.

POSSIBLE PITFALL

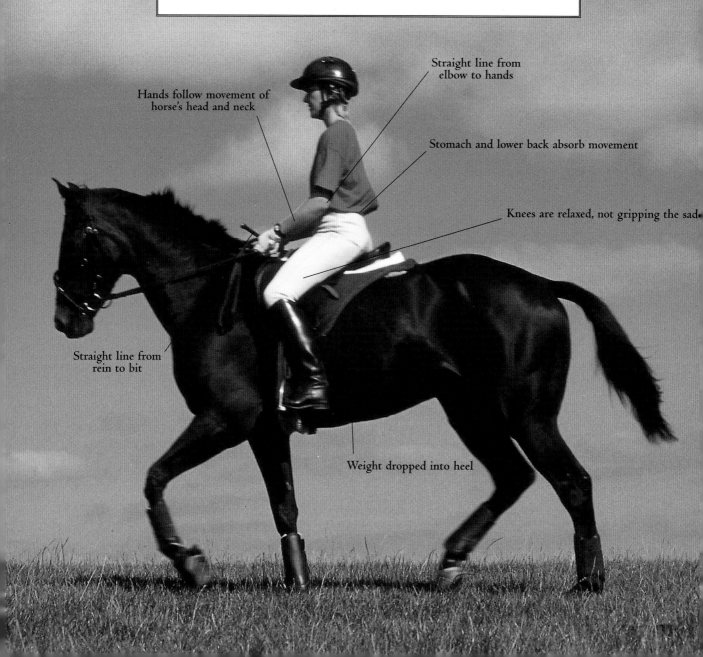

PERFECT POSTURE: SITTING TROT

Because of the increased movement created by the horse in trot, this is one of the hardest paces for the rider to maintain the correct position. You must remain relaxed and allow your lower back and stomach to absorb the up and down motion created by the horse, rather than be bounced up and down by it. The exact position in which you carry your hands is dictated by the position of the horse's head and neck — the hands are carried in the position that allows a straight line to run from the elbow, through the wrist and down the rein to the bit.

Straight line from elbow to hands

Hands follow movement of horse's head and neck

Stomach and lower back absorb movement

Knees are relaxed, not gripping the sad•

Straight line from rein to bit

Weight dropped into heel

TECHNIQUE
SITTING TROT

In sitting trot you should remain sitting deep in the saddle, maintaining the same classical position as when stationary and at walk. The horse's movement is absorbed by your stomach and lower back, so that you stay well in the saddle without being bounced up and down. As you feel the horse's legs springing forwards underneath you, think of allowing your ribcage to sink down towards your hips. This means that the stomach and lower back act like a concertina: as the horse springs along, the stomach and lower back are either contracting or expanding to absorb the movement. You must stay relaxed so that your legs can hang long and loose by the horse's sides, and your arms can maintain a light contact with the horse's mouth. It helps to make a conscious effort to keep breathing — you would be surprised how many riders hold their breath as soon as they concentrate too hard. Steady breathing helps you relax.

2► Keep your knee joints as long and loose as possible during sitting trot.

1◄ Allow your stomach and lower back to absorb the movement. Note the straight line through the shoulder, hip and heel, and from the elbow, down along the rein to the bit.

3◄ Gripping with the knee makes your seat insecure.

POSSIBLE PITFALLS

1◄ Back to the armchair position! How not to sit: the lower leg has slipped forwards and the rider is sitting on the back of her seat. The line from the shoulder through the hip to the heel has also been lost.

2◄ If you fall into the armchair position, your body cannot correctly absorb the movement of the horse. You will be bumped up and down, and as a result, you will find your hands and arms bobbing up and down as well. This is uncomfortable both for you and the horse.

EXERCISE
FROM WALK TO TROT TO WALK

1 ◀ The horse should be walking forwards actively and attentively before you ask for a trot. Keep a contact with the horse's mouth without pulling or restricting him. Your legs must be in contact with the horse's sides without being used actively.

4 ◀ To return to walk, sit deep in the saddle and squeeze your legs against the horse's sides. (If you had been in rising trot, you would return to sitting trot to achieve this.)

2 ◀ To ask for trot, squeeze both legs actively against the horse's sides and soften the hands forwards, so that the horse feels free to increase the pace and go forwards into trot.

5 ◀ Then, instead of softening the hands forwards, keep them still, so that the horse's forward movement is blocked, bringing him back to walk.

3 ◀ Once the horse is settled in trot, your legs and hands return to just being in contact with the horse. The leg is there to squeeze the horse forwards should he slow down, and the hand is there to guide him.

6 ◀ As soon as the horse settles in walk, relax your hands and legs sufficiently to keep just a light contact.

EXERCISE
VARIATIONS ON THE TROT

WORKING TROT

EXTENDED TROT

◄ The working trot is the pace the horse naturally offers the rider. It is an active pace, with the horse maintaining a round outline while working in a forward-thinking rhythm. It is the sort of trot the horse would pro-duce out hacking – relaxed but active. In the extended trot the horse stretches his whole frame and takes steps of maximum length and maximum impulsion, yet remaining balanced

COLLECTED TROT

◄ In the collected paces, which can be either walk, trot or canter, the horse shortens his whole outline by lowering the hindquarters and bringing the hocks further under him, and by elevating the shoulders and forelegs, so that the neck is raised and arched. The horse takes shorter, rounder steps, with greater elevation.

CANTERING

The feeling of speed and power as the horse canters across the ground with each stride is truly exhilarating. But despite the increased speed, riders generally find this a very smooth pace. The canter is a three-time pace, with the legs working in the following sequence: outside hindleg goes forwards, then the inside hindleg and outside foreleg go forwards together, followed by the inside foreleg. There is then a pause, when all four feet are off the ground, before the stride pattern is repeated — outside hind; inside hind and outside fore; then inside fore.

PERFECT POSTURE: CANTER

Again the rider must stick to the golden rules of the classical position; maintaining the ear/shoulder/hip/heel line and the elbow/hand/rein/bit line. In order to keep this position while remaining in balance with the cantering horse, the rider must remain relaxed through her lower back and hips so that these can be rocked gently backwards and forwards by the movement of the horse. Equally the arms must stay soft and relaxed so that they can be drawn forwards by the horse as he moves his head and neck during the canter stride.

Straight line from ear to shoulder

Straight line from elbow to hand

Arms soft and relaxed

Straight line from hip to heel

Lower back relaxed

Hips relaxed

Sit deep in the saddle

Straight line from rein to bit

TECHNIQUE
CANTERING ON THE CORRECT LEG

A horse cantering in a circle should appear to be leading each stride with the inside foreleg. In practice, the inside foreleg is the last leg to be moved, but to the observer it should appear to be the first. When this is the case, the horse is said to be cantering on the correct leg, or the correct lead.

CANTERING ON THE CORRECT REIN
When cantering on the right rein (i.e. circling to the right), the inside (right) foreleg should appear to be leading; and when cantering on the left rein, the inside (left) foreleg appears to be leading.

To ask the horse to canter forwards on the left lead, use the inside leg on the girth and the outside leg behind the girth. Meanwhile, open the left hand slightly to keep the horse bent left, and keep just a feel on the outside rein to stop the horse from simply accelerating in trot. To canter on the right lead the aids are reversed; the right leg is used on the girth, the left leg is used behind the girth, and the right hand is opened slightly to bend the horse to the right.

PERFECT POSTURE
Try to resist the temptation to lean forward in the saddle, dropping your shoulders. This will unbalance the horse and will make the job harder. Keep your seat deep in the saddle and your lower back relaxed.

◄ Cantering on the correct leg. When horse and rider are circling on the left rein, the horse's inside (left) foreleg appears to be leading.

POSSIBLE PITFALLS

1 ◄ Cantering on the wrong leg. Although the horse is still circling to the left, the outside (right) foreleg appears to be leading the stride.

2 ◄ Don't tip forwards and look down over the inside shoulder. As soon as your shoulders drop forwards you are pushed off balance, and your hands tend to drop down on to the horse. You must remain sitting upright and use your hands and legs independently to ask for the transition to canter.

TECHNIQUE
CANTERING IN THE FORWARD SEAT

By lifting your weight out of the saddle, you can encourage the horse to relax his back and put a little more life and swing into his paces. In canter this is often done out on a hack so that the horse is allowed to bowl along effortlessly under the rider.

In a schooling session, the rider may take weight out of the saddle to promote relaxation and help the horse use his back more. This is called riding in the forward seat. You will need to have gained a good sense of balance to do this, and you will also need quite strong leg muscles, as it stretches the backs of the calves. If you feel you are tipping back in the saddle, bring your shoulders slightly further forwards. If you feel you are tipping forwards on to the horse's neck, you should raise your shoulders and check that your lower leg has not slipped backwards, as this in turn pushes your weight forwards.

1 ◄ This rider is sitting firmly in the saddle in the classical position. This is the ideal starting point before you attempt to canter in the forward seat.

2 ◄ Lift your seat bones out of the saddle and allow your weight to sink down into your heels. By removing your weight from the horse's back you will allow him to increase his pace. Do not tip forward or backwards — remain firmly positioned in the centre of the saddle.

AIDS FOR CANTER

It is important to use the correct aids at canter. Problems will occur if the reins are too long and contact with the mouth is lost, or if the legs grip too tightly, so the horse cannot feel the aid given by the legs.

TECHNIQUE
EXTENDED CANTER

This is an advanced pace which is also one of the most enjoyable. A horse is capable of a number of variations of each pace. As the horse's responsiveness to his rider increases, his training progresses and the rider becomes more adept and confident, the horse should be able to offer more power, impulsion and speed. In the extended canter the horse lengthens his frame and fully extends his legs to take the longest possible steps while remaining in a constant rhythm and staying in balance with the rider.

1 ► The rider is positioned firmly in the saddle, maintaining the classical position.

2 ▲ The horse now lengthens his legs, covering more ground as he moves forward.

3 ▲ Here the horse needs to lengthen his neck a little more and take his nose a fraction forwards so that he is not behind the vertical.

TECHNIQUE
COUNTER CANTER

Counter canter tests the horse's balance, suppleness and obedience. It requires the horse to canter with the left leg leading while being worked on the right rein, and vice versa. The horse must keep his head and neck bent over the leading foreleg, so that he is bent in the opposite direction from that in which he is moving.

Introduce counter canter by cantering on the left rein across the diagonal to the opposite track. As the horse reaches the other side and turns on to the right rein, ask him to canter with the left leg leading before bringing him back to trot.

Once you are both comfortable with this, you can ride shallow loops in canter down the long side of an arena; while the horse is on the track he is cantering as normal; while he is negotiating the shallow loop he is in counter canter, provided he maintains the original bend of his head and neck over the leading foreleg.

RIDING A LOOP

1 ▲ The horse canters around the arena on the right rein with the right leg leading as normal. Instead of continuing down the long side of the arena, turn off the track and ride a smooth 5 m (16 ft) loop along the long side. As the horse negotiates the first curve of the loop, he must continue to canter on the right leg.

2 ◄ With his head and neck bent to the right, the horse follows the loop around to the left. He is bent away from the direction in which he is moving. The horse must remain straight – his hindlegs must follow the same tracks as his forelegs, with only his head and neck showing a right bend.

3 ◄ As the horse follows the loop around to the left and back towards the track, he must maintain the canter on the right lead, with his neck bent to the right.

EXERCISE
FROM TROT TO CANTER TO TROT

1▶ Before asking the horse to canter, go into sitting trot and be sure that the horse is working forwards actively and attentively.

2▶ To ask the horse to go forward into canter on the left rein (i.e to canter on the left lead), sit deep, press the inside (left) leg on the girth, but ask more actively with a squeeze of the outside leg back behind the girth. Open your inside hand out slightly to the left to encourage the horse to keep a bend to the left. Your outside hand may have to keep more of a feel than usual on the outside rein to prevent the horse from simply trotting faster.

3▲ Once the correct canter is established, with the inside (left) foreleg apparently leading, keep your outside leg in place behind the girth to encourage the outside hindleg to keep initiating the canter stride. Your inside leg remains on the girth, so that the horse's body is bent around your inside leg as you progress around the circle.

4 ▶ Your arms and hands move forwards with the movement of the horse's head and neck. Sit deep in the saddle, allowing your hips to be rocked by the horse's stride.

5 ▶ To return to trot, sit deep in the saddle and close both legs against the horse's sides.

6 ▶ Reduce the degree to which you allow your hands and arms to move forwards with the horse's head and neck, so that the horse's forward movement is blocked. You may have to keep a slightly stronger feel in the outside hand to help bring the horse back to trot.

7 ▶ As soon as the trot is established, soften your hands forwards again to follow the movement, and allow your legs to hang gently by the horse's sides. Be ready to squeeze the horse forwards again into a more active trot if he tries to slow down any more.

GALLOPING

Riding your horse at the gallop is an invigorating and exciting experience, but to make it safe and enjoyable for you and your horse, you must develop a secure seat and feel confidently in control of the horse. If you lose balance at this pace you will either topple off, or end up hanging on to the reins. The horse will fight this pressure on his mouth, and you may lose control. At this pace, the horse is at full stretch, and to allow him to use himself fully, you should bring your weight up out of the saddle, push your seat further back and tuck your upper body in behind the horse's neck, like a race jockey.

PERFECT POSTURE: GALLOPING

To ride the gallop in balance and safety, the rider should shorten her stirrup leathers so that she is able to lift her seat easily out of the saddle. The rider balances over the horse's withers with her upper body folded forwards and tucked in behind the horse's neck. Here, for the first time the golden rule of the classical position is broken. Once the rider's weight is out of the saddle, the secret to keeping your balance is to imagine a straight line running from the shoulder through the knee to the heel. Your lower leg remains in the normal position.

Upper body tucked behind horse's neck

Shoulders forwards

Straight line from shoulder to knee to heel

Arms extend forwards as horse stretches neck

Body balanced over withers

Seat is out of the saddle

Lower leg remains on girth

Weight dropped down into heels

TECHNIQUE
STOPPING A HARD-PULLING HORSE

It is at the faster paces of canter and gallop that the horse most often becomes over-excited and less responsive to the rider, particularly when it comes to slowing down. While in theory it should be possible to stop a horse at any pace by using the subtle balance of hand and leg, in practice the horse's excitement can override his desire to co-operate.

WHAT TO DO

If you find yourself battling against a pulling horse, make sure your lower leg is pushed forwards whilst still squeezing both legs against the horse's sides. The slightly forward lower leg position allows you to brace yourself against the stirrup. When a horse gets strong, it is easy to be pulled forwards out of the saddle; the lower leg slips back, putting the rider in a very vulnerable position. Shorten up the reins as much as you can, and put one hand, still holding the rein, tight into the horse's neck. Use the other hand to keep a strong hold on the other rein and, by gradually giving and taking this rein, you will help the horse to listen again and slow down. If you keep a continuous pull on the rein, the horse will simply lean on the bit and become stronger still – give and take the rein to prevent him from doing this. Circling the horse will also cause him to slow down.

▶ Notice how the lower leg is pushed forward, yet still in contact with the horse's side. The reins are short, and firmly controlled. Do not pull on the reins. Place a firm hand on the side of the horse's neck to signal to him to slow down.

TECHNIQUE
CURBING HIGH SPIRITS

Most horses enjoy a good gallop and will quite often let their riders know this by popping in a high-spirited leap or buck. If the rider is able to sit this out, it is harmless fun, but it becomes less amusing when it is sufficient to unseat the rider.

KEEPING CONTACT

When cantering or galloping, always keep a contact through the reins with the horse's mouth in order to help balance him. If the horse becomes playful and over-excited, it is even more important to maintain this contact. If the horse throws a playful buck the rider will lose her balance. Often the lower leg slips back and, in order to compensate, the rider balances her weight on her knees rather than securely down in her heel. If the horse continues to play around, the rider will be in a very vulnerable position as it will not take much to dislodge her. To rectify the situation, the rider must get her lower leg further forwards and her weight down in her heel. She will then be more centrally balanced over the horse and more able to stay with him whatever antics he tries next.

LIGHTENING THE LOAD

It sometimes helps to take your weight out of the saddle provided that you do not then lose your lower leg position. You should try to ride the horse forwards up into the contact maintained by your hands on the reins so that you can start to exert some control over what the horse is doing.

◀ Notice how the rider is balancing the horse through the reins. Keep a firm contact with the horse's mouth. Do not pull or tug as this will hurt the horse and may make the situation worse.

◀ It may help to control a wayward horse if you lift your seat out of the saddle. Notice how the leg position remains constant, with the weight down in the heel and pushed slightly forward. This will re-balance the rider's body.

CONTROLLING THE HORSE

There is a subtle difference between learning to ride and actually controlling the horse. You will spend the early period of training simply learning how to sit correctly balanced on the horse and mastering the basic aids that will enable you and your horse to proceed at walk, trot and canter, to halt, and to circle left or right. Until you achieve this balance and the resultant independent seat, you will be little more than a passenger. Once you have acquired an independent seat, you can concern yourself with how well or otherwise your horse is performing underneath you.

TECHNIQUE

INFLUENCING THE HORSE

Use your hands and legs to control and influence the horse's shoulders, hindquarters, head and neck. When making a turn or circling, your legs control the horse's shoulders and hindquarters. Combined with the hands, this can be taken further to move the horse in a number of different ways. You can use your leg behind the girth to encourage the horse to move sideways (laterally) away from the leg, or to control the swing and direction of the quarters. Applying the leg on the girth encourages the horse to bend around the leg, and allows you to control the horse's shoulder.

Once you are able to use each hand and leg independently, without sacrificing your position, balance or control, you will be able to influence the horse's performance fully.

MOVING TO THE RIGHT

1 ◀ Keep a light feel on the outside (left) rein and open the inside hand while pressing the inside leg against the girth, and the horse will bend his head and neck to the right.

2 ▶ If your horse swings his quarters over to the right, straighten him up again by reversing the aids: use the right leg behind the girth to push the quarters back over to the left, while the right hand prevents the horse from stepping forwards.

MOVING TO THE LEFT

1 ◀ While at halt, keep a light feel on the outside (right) rein; open out the inside rein slightly. Squeeze the horse's side with your inside leg on the girth, while the outside leg remains relaxed. The horse will bend his head and neck to the left.

2 ◀ If the horse steps across to the left, straighten up again by pressing your left leg against the girth to push the horse's shoulders back to the right.

TECHNIQUE
LIGHTENING THE FOREHAND

If you watch a horse running loose you will see how proud and active he looks: his neck is high and arched, and he will use his hindquarters to produce round, elevated paces. As soon as an unschooled horse is asked to bear a rider, this picture can change dramatically: the horse's outline becomes flat and long, he may lean on the bit by carrying his head and neck low, or he may carry his head high in an effort to evade the rein and the bit. The rider must teach the horse how to rebalance himself so that he can regain his proud, elegant and light bearing.

THE UNBALANCED HORSE

An unbalanced horse usually takes advantage of the fact that the rider is holding the reins and will lean on the bit, so the rider is helping to carry the weight of the horse. When this happens the horse is said to be on his forehand, i.e. more of the weight of the horse and the rider is carried on the horse's shoulders and forelegs than on the hindquarters and hindlegs.

BALANCING THE HORSE

The horse must carry more of the weight on the hindquarters than on the forehand. In order to do this the horse has to lower the hindquarters and allow the hindlegs to step much further under his body, automatically raising the shoulders, head and neck. This is called lightening the forehand, or transferring the weight from the horse's forehand to the hindquarters.

ENGAGING THE HINDQUARTERS

1 ◄ A young or unschooled horse bearing a rider will present a long, low outline. The head and neck are low, and the overall shape appears long and flat as a result.

2 ◄ Use your legs and seat to encourage the horse to bring the hindlegs further underneath him, and keep just enough contact on the rein to prevent the horse speeding up. The nudge of your legs pushing the horse up into the contact maintained by the hand causes the horse to begin bending and flexing the hocks more, so that they can step further underneath the body. This is known as engaging the hocks or hindquarters.

3 ◀ As the horse undergoes various schooling exercises and also learns to become more responsive to the leg and seat aids, you will gradually be able to encourage the horse to use his hindquarters more. Asking your horse to transfer the weight in this way, from the forehand to the hind-quarters, must always be done by greater use of your legs, not by pulling the horse's head and neck up and in with the reins.

4 ◀ The horse's outline is now more rounded. The forehand has been raised slightly higher than the hind-quarters, so that the horse is carrying more of the weight on the hindquarters and has lightened the forehand. The rein contact should remain soft and elastic, only blocking sufficiently to prevent the horse from speeding up when the leg is applied, instead of engaging the hindquarters more.

TECHNIQUE
LATERAL WORK

Once you are able to send the horse forwards into walk, trot, canter and gallop, and are able to halt, you are ready to learn how to make the horse move sideways — either with the whole body or just the shoulders or hindquarters. This is known as lateral work, and is invaluable in teaching a novice to feel and influence the horse's movement. For the horse, it is a useful suppling exercise and an encouragement to work more actively with the hindquarters.

Lateral movements include leg yielding, quarters-in (both described here), and shoulder-in and half-pass. All horses should be introduced to these exercises, and to backward movement (see Rein Back) as part of their overall training programme. Practise them at walk. When you have mastered control of the shoulders and hindquarters, you will realize just how manoeuvrable the horse can be.

LEG YIELDING
The horse is asked to move forwards and sideways at the same time; the inside hindleg and foreleg cross over in front of the outside hindleg and foreleg.

When the horse leg yields, he keeps his body bent away from the direction in which he is being asked to move, i.e. his body is bent to the right but he is moving away to the left.

1 ◀ To leg yield across to the left, bring your right leg behind the girth, which tells the horse to move sideways; keep the left leg on the girth, asking the horse to keep moving forwards as well as sideways. Open the right hand a few inches, which encourages the horse to maintain a slight right bend through the body; the left hand should keep sufficient feel on the rein to prevent the horse from bending too far to the left; combined with the push from the right leg behind the girth, it invites the horse to step sideways.

2 ▶ The rider's right leg is used just behind the girth to ask the horse to move sideways rather than forwards. The left hand invites the horse to step sideways to the left. The left leg is used on the girth to ask the horse to keep moving forwards as well, whilst the right hand maintains the bend to the right. To leg yield away to the right, reverse the aids: use the left leg behind the girth, the right leg on the girth, the right rein keeping enough contact to invite the horse to step to the right, and the left rein opening a few inches to encourage the horse to keep a slight bend through the body.

TECHNIQUE
QUARTERS-IN

For this technique, the horse continues walking in a straight line but brings the quarters in to one side. If you imagine the horse walking on sand, the horse's hoofprints would leave three lines of tracks: the inside line formed by the inside hindleg; the middle line made by the inside fore and the outside hindlegs (which follow each other); and the outside line made by the outside foreleg.

BASIC PRINCIPLES OF CONTROL

Before you and your horse can work effectively and happily together, there are a number of basic principles that you both have to master. These form the basis of all horses' training and progression, whether or not they have been properly schooled. Once you have mastered these principles, you will be equipped with the means to ride your horse to the maximum of his potential.

- Acceptance of rein contact
- Free forward movement
- Maintaining a rhythm
- Bend and flexion through the body
- The use of half-halts (see the Half-Halt) to engage the hindquarters and rebalance the horse

---

I ◀ This is a good exercise to increase suppleness in the horse and also teaches the rider how to use a combination of hand and leg aids to move the horse in different ways. To bring the quarters in to the left, as here use your outside (right) leg behind the girth to move the quarters across slightly. Your inside leg stays on the girth to prevent the shoulders moving out of line. Opening the left hand slightly, combined with the pressure from the left leg on the girth, encourages the horse to keep a bend through his whole body. Take up enough of a feel with the outside hand to keep the horse's shoulder moving forwards in a straight line.

2 ▶ The rider has used her right leg behind the girth to push the horse's hindquarters over to the right. Her left leg remains on the girth and asks the horse to keep moving forwards. The right hand controls the horse's right shoulder – keeping it moving forwards on a straight line. Quarters-in to the right is achieved by reversing the aids: use the left leg behind the girth; keep the right leg (now the inside leg) on the girth, open the right hand slightly; and with the left (outside) hand take up enough of a feel to keep the horse's shoulders moving forward in a straight line.

TECHNIQUE
REIN BACK

The rein back means asking the horse to walk backwards. For safety it should only ever be performed in walk – although, when frightened, a horse is quite capable of running backwards at a respectable speed!

Although the rein back is not, of course, a lateral movement, it belongs to the practice, for horse and rider, of learning the full extent of the control and motion they can achieve.

The horse should step backwards in a straight line, moving the legs clearly and positively in diagonal pairs: inside foreleg and outside hindleg together, followed by outside fore and inside hind together.

Because the legs are applied actively, the horse knows he has to move somewhere. The rein contact is telling him he cannot go forwards and so he goes backwards. Some horses understand what is required more easily if you apply legs behind the girth and lift your seat bones out of the saddle. This encourages the horse to step back underneath you as required.

OBEDIENCE TEST

Rein back is sometimes used to test the obedience and suppleness of a horse. Some horses may be reluctant to move backwards, and may arch their backs or drop their heads, so it is also a good opportunity to test your use of aids. You should keep a good, constant contact with your legs and hands.

1 ◀ The rein back can only be performed successfully if the horse is calm and relaxed when at the halt.

2 ▶ Squeeze both legs against the horse's sides, but make sure that you block the horse's forward movement by preventing your hands from moving forwards. Apply both legs behind the girth, and then lift your seat bones off the saddle, as demonstrated here.

3 ◀ After taking a step back with one diagonal pair of legs, the horse proceeds to step back with the remaining diagonal pair. You should only ask the horse to step backwards for a limited number of steps. As a reward, allow him to walk forwards again while making a fuss over him.

TECHNIQUE
ACCEPTANCE OF CONTACT

The horse has to learn to accept that the bit in his mouth is attached, via the reins, to the rider's hands, and that there will always be a contact between the two. It is vital that you achieve a balanced, independent seat, so that you are not tempted to hang on to the reins in an effort to balance yourself. Your priority is to learn to follow the movement of the horse's head and neck so that you are able to keep a constant but sympathetic contact with his mouth. In the early stages of training, do not concern yourself with how the horse is carrying his head and neck, but only with learning to feel, follow and maintain the contact. Once the horse knows that the contact is constant, but kind, he will learn to accept it without resentment. To keep the right contact, your elbows must remain soft and relaxed. It may be necessary to open your hands a little wider than usual so that there is no obstruction – whatever the horse does with his head, you can follow it with your hands.

FOLLOWING THE HORSE'S HEAD AND NECK

1 ◄ Do not worry too much about the position of the horse's head and neck in the early stages of training. Concentrate on learning to follow their movement, so that you maintain a soft but constant contact, through the reins, with the mouth.

2 ◄ If the horse rears his head upwards, relax your grip on the reins and follow the movement.

POSSIBLE PITFALLS

1 ◄ This rider is not maintaining the contact and has lost communication with the horse – who is now ignoring her leg and hand aids. He will continue to plod along lethargically until the rider reminds him to listen to the hand and leg.

2 ◄ The horse must respond the same way in all paces. This horse is in trot, but again, the contact and communication have been lost. The rider is working hard with her legs whilst the horse is being extremely lazy with his!

RESPONDING TO HAND AND LEG

TECHNIQUE
FREE FORWARD MOVEMENT

The horse must learn to respect the rider's legs. When you use your legs against the horse's sides, he must respond – by going forwards if you apply both legs together, or by moving away from the leg that you use as a lateral aid. The vast majority of problems experienced by riders are caused by the horse ignoring, or being slow to reply to, the leg aids. The horse's first reaction should always be to move forwards. Once the horse respects the leg and is willing to maintain free forward movement without your continually having to reapply the leg aids, he is said to be in front of the leg and on the aids – he is attentive and ready to react instantly to your commands.

USING AIDS
If the horse is slow to respond, use a combination of aids, voice, legs, heels and schooling whip. Be ready to allow movement with the hands, particularly if the horse jumps forward when the schooling whip is used. As soon as the horse moves forwards, reward him by praising him verbally. Gradually the horse will learn to respond to the first light aid.

Mastering soft contact through the reins with the horse's mouth will make free forward movement easier. Remember that these movements should be gentle. The horse's mouth, like the human mouth, is a sensitive area and should be treated with care.

1 ◄ Shorten the reins sufficiently to keep a light contact with the horse's mouth. Apply the legs, backed up with a tap from the schooling whip only if necessary. The picture here, as the horse responds, is already one of greater alertness and activity.

2 ◄ Maintain the soft contact and squeeze the legs once more to ask the horse to walk on a little more energetically. If the horse does not respond instantly, use your voice to urge him on, or back up your leg action with a sharp nudge with both heels against the horse's side.

3 ◄ This time, the horse responds instantly. Then your leg can relax and the horse will preserve the forward movement without further nagging. Note how the horse's outline is now much rounder and shorter as he begins to lighten his forehand.

4 ◀ In trot, take up contact with the horse's mouth and back up your leg aids with a tap from the schooling whip.

5 ▶ Immediately the horse offers much more in the way of forward impulsion. Now that he is thinking forwards, he lengthens his steps and voluntarily raises his head and neck into a rounder, shorter outline.

6 ◀ You can then relax your legs and enjoy the forward movement that the horse is offering you. But as soon as the horse drops back from this pace, you must start the process over again.

TECHNIQUE
SHOULDER-IN

The following technique encourages active and effective use of the hocks. It teaches the horse suppleness, to respond to different hand and leg aids, and to place the hocks further underneath him so as to carry more of his body weight on the hindquarters than on the forehand.

SHOULDER-IN

The shoulder-in is similar to quarters-in, in that the horse moves on three tracks, but here it is the shoulders that are brought in, not the quarters, as the horse continues to move forwards. The footfalls are as follows: the inside track is made by the inside foreleg; the middle track by the outside foreleg and inside hindleg together; and the outside track is made by the outside hindleg.

It is quite difficult in shoulder-in for the new rider to keep the horse moving in a straight line. The horse may try to swing his quarters out one way, or may drift sideways. If you are working in an arena, it helps to do the following: as you bring the horse's shoulders in off the track, make sure you are looking ahead yourself. Think of your outside hip as a pointer; if you imagine keeping your hip moving forwards in a straight line, the horse's outside shoulder will move forwards on the same line. The correct position in shoulder-in is for your hips to stay parallel with the horse's shoulders, but for your shoulders to be held straight. You should look straight ahead and keep your head still.

1 ◄ Here, the rider is about to ride shoulder-in in trot down the long side of the arena. She has already ridden a 10 m (33 ft) circle in trot in the corner that she is just coming from. To start the shoulder-in, go to ride another 10 m (33 ft) circle, but as soon as the horse's front legs have left the track to start the circle, use the outside hand to prevent his continuing on the circle, and the inside leg to keep him moving forwards along the side of the arena. To keep the horse moving forwards in a straight line while in shoulder-in, look straight ahead and think of your outside hip as pointing the way forwards.

2 ▲ As the horse progresses down the long side of the arena in shoulder-in, it can be seen how he is working on three tracks (inside fore, outside fore/inside hind, outside hind). This exercise encourages the horse to be supple, because he has to maintain a bend through his body and neck; it also introduces the horse to the idea of carrying more weight on the inside hindleg. Note that as the inside hindleg touches the ground, it is placed directly under the horse's belly and beneath the rider. So at this point the horse is carrying much of his body weight, as well as the weight of the rider, on that inside hindleg.

3 ▲ To help keep the horse moving forwards in a straight line while in shoulder-in, the rider should look straight ahead and think of her outside hip as pointing the way forwards.

TECHNIQUE
THE HALF-PASS

In half-pass the horse moves diagonally across the arena, taking good-sized steps forwards and sideways, and keeping the body bent in the direction in which he is moving. The shoulders are allowed to be just fractionally ahead of the hindquarters as the horse makes this movement. The outside hindleg and foreleg cross over in front of the inside hindleg and foreleg.

THE EASY OPTION

The horse may often try to make life easier for himself by not maintaining the correct bend. He may bend his body to the outside, which means, in effect, that he is simply leg yielding. To correct this, you should ride the horse forwards in a straight line, so that he knows immediately that his response was not acceptable. Re-establish shoulder-in, and use the outside leg to bring the quarters over and keep the horse stepping sideways. As soon as the horse offers the wrong bend again, ride him forwards in a straight line and repeat the process. You may need to tap the horse with the schooling whip just behind the inside leg to make sure he is listening to that leg and remains bent around it.

1 ◀ To ride the half-pass, shown here in walk, turn down the long side of the arena and ask the horse to go into shoulder-in. Instead of continuing in shoulder-in, use the outside leg back behind the girth to push the horse's hindquarters across until they are almost directly in line with the shoulders. Your outside leg stays in place, telling the horse to move sideways, while the inside leg also keeps him moving forwards. Your outside hand controls the degree of bend through the horse's body and neck, while the inside hand remains open, inviting the horse to step forwards and sideways.

2 ▶ In half-pass, the horse must remain bent around your inside leg, in the direction in which he is moving. As shown here, your outside leg works behind the girth to push the horse sideways. Half-pass can be ridden in walk, trot and canter.

3 ◀ This picture shows the horse working in half-pass to the left. You can see that it is the outside hindleg that must come across and under the horse, taking the weight of both horse and rider. The exercise encourages suppleness in the horse, particularly through the shoulders.

TECHNIQUE
RHYTHM AND BALANCE

When the horse accepts the contact and moves forward willingly from your leg, you both need to acquire an even rhythm in all you do. This rhythm must not be too slow, or the work will lack impulsion and power; neither must it be too fast, or the horse will become unbalanced and will be pushed on to the forehand. Aim for a rhythm in each pace which gives you the feeling of free forward movement without being rushed. Use a light squeeze from the legs to ride the horse up into this rhythm; then enjoy the experience while the horse maintains the rhythm without continual nagging from hand or leg.

USING AIDS
Once the horse responds quickly to the leg, you are halfway there. Some horses will automatically assume a steady rhythm. Others will need a reminder from leg, voice or schooling whip to keep up to the rhythm, or may need to be slowed down. Do not dampen your horse's goodwill by restricting him with the reins if he goes too fast. The use of a neck strap to slow the horse is a better method; it prevents the horse from learning how to lean on the bit or to fight you by shortening and tensing his neck.

Pulling on the neck strap instead of blocking with the reins will slow the horse. Practise in the arena, first using the strap to bring the horse from walk to halt, and then from trot to walk, etc. Once the horse understands this method, it can be employed to steady him within any pace.

USING THE NECK STRAP

1 ◀ Introduce the neck strap to slow the horse's pace: here, to bring the horse back from trot to walk. Put the reins in one hand and hold the neck strap in the other.

2 ▶ Squeeze your legs lightly against the horse's sides, while using your voice and a firm pull on the neck strap to slow him down. Although you want to slow the horse, you must apply the leg because it encourages the horse to bring the hindlegs further underneath him and therefore keep the forehand light. If you do not use the leg, the horse will simply shift his weight on to the forehand and become heavy and unbalanced in your hand.

3 ◄ The horse comes back quite happily to walk without the need to block with the rein. Remember to reward him with a pat and some praise.

4 ► When working in trot, if the horse has a tendency to speed up out of the desired rhythm, you can just loop a finger through the neck strap and take a pull on it until the horse slows the rhythm again.

5 ◄ When the horse responds, release the neck strap and praise him.

TECHNIQUE
BEND AND FLEXION

In riding you must strive to ensure that the horse's hindlegs follow in the same tracks as the front legs. This is referred to as straightness in the horse, a term that is confusing. For the horse to be straight (i.e. for the hindlegs to follow in the same tracks as the forelegs) while working on a turn or a circle, the horse must bend through the body in a continual curve around the rider's inside leg. So in order to be straight, the horse has to bend!

DEVELOPING BEND AND FLEXION

With time and practice, you will find that the horse will become more and more responsive to the request to bend and flex. After a while, you will not need to open the inside hand in such an exaggerated fashion; simply moving the hand over a couple of centimetres (about an inch) will be sufficient. Much further down the line it will also only be necessary to take up a feel on the inside rein and to close the legs against the horse's sides to achieve bend and flexion.

Once bend and flexion are established in trot, you can strive for the same result in both walk and canter. In all cases, always reward the horse by softening the inside hand the instant that he offers you even the tiniest degree of flexion and relaxation. The horse may only offer you the bend and flexion for a few strides before you have to repeat the process, but as he begins to understand what is wanted, he will offer it to you for longer periods. Gradually you will be doing less asking and more rewarding. But you will need to be persistent and consistent in your training.

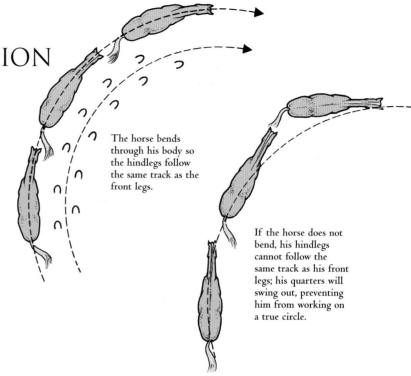

The horse bends through his body so the hindlegs follow the same track as the front legs.

If the horse does not bend, his hindlegs cannot follow the same track as his front legs; his quarters will swing out, preventing him from working on a true circle.

◀ As the horse bends his body, he brings his hocks well underneath him. The hind-quarters are lowered slightly, and the poll and jaw are relaxed, so that the front of the face is on the vertical.

ACHIEVING BEND AND FLEXION

1 ◄ Make sure that the outside hand is following the horse's movement in a soft way, while maintaining a light contact. This ensures that the horse's forward momentum is not stifled by a restricting outside hand. Then open the inside hand, setting it in the open position simply by tensing the muscles of the arm, not by pulling back on the rein. Use the inside leg on the girth to keep the horse pushed out on to the circle, and take up a firmer contact only on the outside rein if the horse falls in on the circle. If he does this, keep pushing the horse out with the inside leg and draw him back on to the original circle by using the outside rein.

2 ► You should now feel the horse bending through the body and neck; if the horse resists and does not offer some bend through the body, simply open the inside rein out further and set it there – still without pulling back on it. Keep the inside leg on, and back it up with a tap from the schooling whip if the horse continues to fall in on the circle rather than bending through the body.

3 ◄ As soon as you can see a glimpse of his inside eye and nostril, use both legs to bring his hocks further underneath and to flex through his topline. When you feel the horse relax his poll and jaw, soften the inside rein and allow it to follow the movement in the same way as the outside rein. The horse is now beginning to work in self-carriage, i.e. he is carrying more weight on the hindquarters and is lightening the forehand.

TECHNIQUE

THE RIGHT DEGREE OF BEND

The degree of bend that the horse shows through his body depends on the size of circle or turn you are riding. To ride a 20 m (65 ft) circle, for example, the horse shows only a slight bend, but to manoeuvre around a 10 m (33 ft) circle, there will be a greater degree of bend.

DEGREES OF BEND

The more the horse has to bend the body, the more he has to use the hocks; the inside hindleg, in particular, must step further across and under the horse's body. Having ridden simple turns and circles, you will know that the inside leg is used on the girth with an open inside hand to encourage the horse to bend around the inside leg, while the outside leg is used back behind the girth to prevent the quarters swinging out. The outside hand prevents the horse bending his head and neck too much to the inside.

FLEXING THROUGH THE TOPLINE

Once the horse is willing to offer you the bend through his whole body, you can ask him to flex through his topline so that his whole outline becomes soft and he offers you no resistance. When this is achieved, the hindquarters are lowered as the hocks come further underneath him, he stays soft through the back, arches the neck, and relaxes the poll and jaw, so that the head is carried in a relaxed manner; the horse will lower his nose, so that a vertical line could be drawn from the front of his face to the ground.

OBTAINING THE CORRECT DEGREE OF BEND

1 ◄ You should only ask for a slight bend through the horse's body and neck, so that the outside of the horse makes a continual curve around your inside leg. You only need to see a glimpse of the horse's inside eye and nostril to know that the degree of bend is correct.

2 ◄ As soon as the horse responds to your aids by bending through the body and then flexing through the topline, soften the inside hand and praise the horse as a reward. This is the only way that the horse can know that he has responded to the aids in the right way.

3 ► While you are softening your inside hand, you can also use it to pat the horse's neck in further praise.

4 ◄This horse is offering the required degree of bend and flexion. Note the arch of the neck and how the forehand appears lighter and higher than the hindquarters. The horse is really flexing the hock as he goes to step forwards with the hindleg. Most importantly, the rider has softened the inside rein, so that the horse is holding this outline himself.

POSSIBLE PITFALLS

1 ►A frequent difficulty is for the horse to bend only through the neck from the withers, so that the body remains straight. In this position the horse can avoid having to step under himself more with the hindlegs, so the quarters will swing out as he goes around a corner. If the hocks are not underneath him, the horse can neither turn correctly nor flex through the topline when asked. You must use the outside rein to reduce the degree of bend in the neck, and the outside leg to keep the hindquarters from swinging out, and you should reinforce the inside leg by tapping the horse with the schooling whip behind the lower leg.

2 ◄Another pitfall occurs when the horse tilts his head towards the inside. He allows your inside hand to draw his nose to the inside but ignores the outside hand, so instead of bending through the neck and poll, he simply tilts his head to one side. Take up more contact with the outside rein to correct this.

TECHNIQUE
THE HALF-HALT

The half-halt describes what happens when you close your legs and hands momentarily against the horse. This serves to rebalance the horse in whatever pace he is working; your legs push the horse's hindlegs further underneath him while your hand blocks any acceleration in pace which the horse might offer. The power that the legs have created is trapped by your hand, so that instead of accelerating, the horse lowers the hind-quarters and elevates the forehand slight-ly, becoming better balanced and lighter in your hand. The half-halt can be used to (1) rebalance the horse in any pace; (2) warn the horse that you are about to ask him to do something, such as change direction; and (3) build impulsion with-in each pace, which can be stored to produce collected work, or released to produce extended work.

THE HALF-HALT AT WALK
First, practise the half-halt at walk. At a given point, close your legs against the horse's sides and reduce the degree to which you allow your hands to follow the contact, as if you were going to halt. Just as you sense the horse is about to halt, soften your hands forward again, keeping your legs on the horse's sides, so that he continues in walk. Once you get the feel of how much leg and hand is needed to produce this effect of almost but not quite halting the horse, you will have achieved a half-halt.

HALF-HALT AT TROT

1 ◀ This horse is producing an active trot, and is maintaining a good outline; although he is only young, the overall picture is soft and round. It is sufficient to sit quietly with the leg aid on, and maintain a light contact with the reins to the horse's mouth.

2 ◀ Now the horse is becoming unbalanced. He has probably over-powered himself with the push from his hindlegs and is poking his nose forward and starting to lean on the bit in an attempt to balance himself. The soft, round outline is disappearing.

3 ◄ A half-halt is needed to rebalance the horse. Close your legs on the horse's sides and push him up into your hand which, just for a second, is blocked against the horse's forward movement. In effect, the horse's body is squashed up; his outline becomes shorter because the hindlegs are pushed further under the body. The horse is therefore able to carry more weight on the hindlegs, which in turn lightens and elevates the forehand.

4 ◄ Reward the horse by relaxing the leg and softening the hand. The softening of the rein has been exaggerated in this picture to show that once the horse is using the hindquarters and hocks more actively, he is able to carry himself and remain light in the rider's hand. So although the rein is completely loose, the horse is maintaining his own balance and a correct outline.

TECHNIQUE
THE HALF HALT AT CANTER

Every horse will respond to a combination of hand and leg. You have to find out what combination is needed for your horse to obtain the desired result. Too much hand and the horse will either resist by throwing his head up, or will simply slow down. Too much leg and the horse will try to accelerate and be pushed on to the forehand, which will unbalance him.

Practise the half-halt at trot and at canter. Each time, act as if to bring the horse back to the slower pace and, at the last second, allow him to continue in the original pace. Once you have mastered the half-halt, you can use it more subtly to forewarn the horse that you are about to ask him to do something different.

1 ◀ This horse is falling on to the forehand at canter. His weight appears to be dropping forwards and he seems to be leaning on the bit, and therefore on the rider's hands, for support.

2 ◀ You can use a half-halt to rebalance the horse. Close your legs against the horse's sides and block any forward acceleration with your hands.

3 ▶ The horse will become balanced and light in your hands. In picture one the hindquarters appeared higher than the shoulders (on the forehand). Now the shoulders are higher than the hindquarters (the forehand is elevated and lightened).

POSSIBLE PITFALL

1 ◄ Here the rider has tried to rebalance the canter by raising and pulling back with the hands.

2 ► Notice too how she has provided no back-up from the leg.

3 ◄ The result is that the horse responds by simply falling back into the trot.

PUTTING IT ALL TOGETHER

ACHIEVING COLLECTION AND EXTENSION OF THE PACES

Producing variations within each pace involves bringing together the techniques and principles shown in this book. Whether the horse is working in the collected, medium or extended paces, he must maintain the same rhythm. In other words, you do not slow the horse down in order to achieve collection, nor should you go faster in order to extend the horse.

HOW TO DO IT

To achieve collection, use the half-halt to bring the horse's hocks further underneath him while your hand prevents him from accelerating. Because your hand traps the power produced by the use of the leg, the horse shortens his frame and puts that power into taking shorter, higher steps. To carry out medium or extended work, first use half-halts to collect the horse, and then release that power and energy in varying degrees by softening the hand forwards, which enables the horse to lengthen his frame and his stride. Whether the resulting pace is medium or extended depends on the degree to which you soften with the hand while continuing to ask for more power and drive from the hindquarters.

To be able to produce these variations in pace, you have to develop a good feel for creating and storing energy for collected work, and for directing that energy forwards into medium or extended work.

COLLECTING AND EXTENDING THE PACES

1 ◀ It is best to work in an arena for this exercise. The short side which provides two nearby corners is a good place to ask for collection; the horse has to bring the inside hindleg further underneath him to negotiate the turn anyway. The diagonal provides room for extending the paces. Use half-halts to collect the horse as you progress through the corner of the arena and begin to turn across the diagonal.

2 ◀ As the horse starts to cross the diagonal, continue to collect the energy that was built up as you came through the turn. The horse's outline remains relatively high and short.

3◄ Once the horse is completely straight, ask him to extend. Continue to ask for impulsion and drive from the hindquarters by keeping your legs actively on the horse's sides, but now release that stored power by softening the hands forwards, so that the horse can lengthen his frame and strides. Note how the horse's hindquarters are still lowered, and how the first surge of released energy has really elevated his front end as he begins to extend his steps.

4◄ The outline is now lower and longer as the horse extends his limbs forwards to cover as much ground as possible with each stride.

INDEX